MW00936407

DEPRESSION
IN THE CHURCH

Is It Spiritual, Or Is It Physical?

ALISON K. HALL

WESTBOW·
PRESS
A DIVISION OF THOMAS NELSON
& ZONDERVAN

Epigraph from *Why Do Christians Shoot Their Wounded?* by Dwight L. Carlson. Copyright (c) 1994 Dwight L. Carlson. Used by permission of InterVarsity Press, PO Box 1400, Downers Grove, IL 60515. www.ivpress.com

Scripture taken from the King James Version of the Bible.

Scriptures taken from the Holy Bible, New International Version®, NIV®. Copyright © 1973, 1978, 1984, 2011 by Biblica, Inc.™ Used by permission of Zondervan. All rights reserved worldwide. www.zondervan.com The "NIV" and "New International Version" are trademarks registered in the United States Patent and Trademark Office by Biblica, Inc.™ All rights reserved.

When indicated, comments by Matthew Henry were taken from *Matthew Henry's Commentary on the Whole Bible: Complete and Unabridged* by Matthew Henry, copyright 1997 by Hendrickson Publishers, Peabody, Massachusetts. Used by permission. All rights reserved.

WestBow Press books may be ordered through booksellers or by contacting:

WestBow Press
A Division of Thomas Nelson & Zondervan
1663 Liberty Drive
Bloomington, IN 47403
www.westbowpress.com
1 (866) 928-1240

Because of the dynamic nature of the Internet, any web addresses or links contained in this book may have changed since publication and may no longer be valid. The views expressed in this work are solely those of the author and do not necessarily reflect the views of the publisher, and the publisher hereby disclaims any responsibility for them.

Cover photo by Alison K. Hall

ISBN: 978-1-4908-3388-0 (sc)
ISBN: 978-1-4908-3389-7 (hc)
ISBN: 978-1-4908-3387-3 (e)
Library of Congress Control Number: 2014906639

Printed in the United States of America.

WestBow Press rev. date: 04/24/2014

CONTENTS

This book is dedicated to those who have silently struggled with depression. You are not alone.

The widespread nature of Christianity's prejudice can be seen in churches across the nation on any Sunday morning. In most of our churches we pray publicly for the parishioner with cancer, a heart attack, or pneumonia. But rarely will a conservative church publicly pray for Mary with severe depression, Charles with incapacitating panic attacks, or the minister's son with schizophrenia. Such a conspiracy of silence further communicates that these are not acceptable illnesses for Christians to have. And by our silence we further wound those in pain.

—Dwight L. Carlson,
Why Do Christians Shoot Their Wounded?

PREFACE

We had just walked down to the beach. The wind was stronger than it had been all week. "You're not going to want to put your umbrella up today," said a woman just leaving. "It's too windy. I feel like I've been sandblasted!" The whitecaps started far out into the ocean, and the waves roared as they sprayed and crashed onto the sand. The foreboding sky seemed to warn us to stay alert. It was the last day of our summer vacation. *We'll just stay an hour,* I thought.

"Play in the surf today; don't go beyond the breaking waves," we warned our four children as they eagerly ran into the water. Repeatedly, the boys were pulled up the beach. They'd get out to run toward us and then get back in to resume their game of wrestling in the water.

At one point, I looked up the beach to where our two oldest boys were playing. The water was retreating, which lured the boys farther out. With the water at waist level, they felt safe and continued rollicking in the waves. The surf had dragged the kids farther out than they realized. The water seemed manageable at waist level, but I knew it would quickly surge back, swallowing them up in the powerful waves.

Getting out of my chair, I started jogging down the beach with my eyes fixed on their now bobbing heads. As the water quickly moved in, Hunter's head disappeared under the breaking waves. When his head reappeared, it was obvious he was being pulled out.

Running now, I charged into the water. Through the crashing waves I saw my terrified son, who was screaming, "*Help!*"

My oldest son was closest. "Grab him!" I yelled just as a huge wave crashed down on both of us. Recovering his senses, Robbie reached out to grab Hunter. We fought the waves all the while the pull of the ocean was dragging us backward. We crawled out of the water exhausted and shaken.

This scene reminds me of my first encounter with depression. About nine years ago, after my third son was born, I found myself being pulled out into a very dark and powerful storm. I was struggling against a growing number of nebulous ailments, drowning without anyone to run out and get me. I felt rejected by God.

I read the Bible. I prayed. I confessed all my sins, even some I am not sure I did, just trying to win back God's favor. I found myself sinking, getting pulled out to sea, fighting for my very life. Desperately searching for help—books, materials, answers—I was dismayed to find there was very little available. The sparse amount of help compounded my discouragement.

As Christians, we like to see how other people weather difficult storms. We gather strength and encouragement from their stories. I have wanted to share my story for a long time in order to open up a discussion about Christians with depression and God's faithfulness to them in their storms.

ACKNOWLEDGEMENTS

Thank You, Jesus, for carrying me; I would not have made it on my own. I would like to thank my husband, Robert, for being there for me; I am so thankful for you. I want to thank my parents, Leon and Kathy. Your lives of faithful service to the Lord have taught me that He is faithful. You were never in doubt of God's love for me. Thank you, Robbie Jr., Hunter, Matthew, and Lizzie, for making me laugh and for forgiving so easily. I want to thank my parents-in-law, Bobby and Carolyn, for giving up their time to help and support our family. To Sandy, Tim, Gillian, Meredith, and Leah, thank you for supporting me; you were always on my side. Thank you, Cathy, Christy, Dawn, Kristen, my Panera group—Janet, Janice, Sandy, Sue, Tara, Tina, Bev—and all my friends; you loved me even though you didn't understand.

INTRODUCTION

What is a Christian to do? You tell your pastor you are discouraged and feel hopeless and guilty. You feel like God has totally rejected you, like his finger of judgment is pointing right at you, squashing you. You are having disturbing thoughts. You feel oppressed and it frightens you. You feel it is all your fault. You can't sleep, you're having headaches, and you lose your appetite. Your pastor may compassionately point you to Job or Psalms. Maybe you've just experienced a loss or a disappointment. Perhaps you have sin in your life you need to deal with. He might encourage you, pray with you, and give you some Scriptures to read.

You recount the same list of symptoms to your doctor. He tells you that you have depression and that it needs to be treated. He may order some blood work. He may give you a prescription to try.

Which is it? Who is right? Who do you even ask for advice? What will your Christian friends or your pastor think if they find out you are taking an antidepressant? That seems so unspiritual. You feel like you want to lock yourself in your house until it all goes away, but it doesn't. It gets much worse.

What is depression? Is it being spiritually discouraged? Is it a physical illness that affects your brain and your body? What happens when your symptoms don't go away? What do other Christians think about depression? What does God think about depression? There are many questions around the issue of depression and many different answers coming from the Christian community. Do we really understand the issue well enough to give a simple answer?

Let's stop right here. This is the fog that has been hovering around the mainstream Christian community in America for far too long. When I have heard the topic addressed over Christian radio or from Christian leadership in general, the message seems to be clouded at best, but the predominant theme is that depression is a spiritual issue.

Please join me as I share my journey through physical depression. My goal is threefold. First, I hope that any brother or sister struggling with depression can pick up this book and find comfort, hope, and a place to feel understood. Secondly, I intend to identify the schemes the Devil uses to confuse and devastate Christian families struggling with depression. Third, I want to challenge the church to reevaluate its position, and the message it is sending about depression to Christians and non-Christians alike.

As ambassadors for Jesus Christ, our response to this issue could mean life or death for someone struggling with depression. It's an issue we all need to take a long, hard look at.

CHAPTER ONE

My Story

I'm a fourth-generation Christian on my mother's side and a fifth-generation Christian on my father's side. Before I was born, my parents had committed themselves to walking with Jesus. I'd watch my parents get up before the sun and spend time in God's Word. They stood on conviction and suffered for it. I saw that as my parents honored God's Word, His faithfulness gave them joy and strength. Hebrews 1:6 states, "And without faith it is impossible to please God, because anyone who comes to him must believe that he exists and that he rewards those who earnestly seek him." I wanted to live my life that way.

I went to college and got my bachelor's degree in science and nursing. My first job was as a nurse in a telemetry unit, working with cardiac patients. There was an elderly patient I'll never forget. After a successful open-heart surgery, he became depressed. He stayed in our unit during his electroconvulsive therapy treatments, and the staff became attached to him. He wouldn't eat, which threw off his electrolytes, and then he was unable to have his treatments. His death from the complication of depression puzzled me, but would become more clear years later.

In 1998, I married my husband, Robert. It was then that I started taking my personal walk of faith seriously. We attended a Bible church and became involved in different ministries. Robert was on the deacon board and helped with technical and computer issues for the church. We served in the communion ministry. I worked in Awana and in Sunday school.

We had our first child, Robbie Jr., in 2000. Our second son, Hunter, came two years later. In June 2004, Matthew was born. We felt very blessed to have three healthy boys, a wonderful, supportive family, and good friends at church.

My first symptoms of depression came on so slowly that I attributed them to the exhaustion of motherhood. Late-night feedings, early-morning feedings, crying baby, crying toddlers, crying mother … didn't those happen in every house?

It was when Matthew was about three months old that I had my first strange thought. One September afternoon, I sat nursing Matthew on the couch, looking down at his cute little face. I had the strangest sense that he was laughing at me. I shook my head. He was making fun of me, I thought. Knowing that this sounded crazy, I kept it to myself.

I began having a lot of difficulty making decisions. Even the most insignificant decisions became stressful. I second-guessed everything. Any suggestion or complaint felt like a mountain crushing me. It seemed like a heavy hand was pressing down on me. I was exhausted.

By October, I was having difficulty remembering things. I found myself standing in the grocery store one day, as if I had just woken up. I had no idea how long I'd been standing there. I would walk around my house saying to myself, "Okay, so what am I doing?" I could not focus. All my thoughts seemed to be stuck behind me. I couldn't get them in front of me.

I had been having my devotions all along, but I thought maybe I would get up earlier and really try to focus on God's Word. The more I tried, the more frustrated I became.

I was afraid to be left alone with the kids. Something was wrong, and I didn't know where the edge was. I didn't recognize myself and began to feel detached. My mental compass had melted into four limp strings of spaghetti, all pointing down. I lost all my bearings.

Around the middle of October, I began having disturbing thoughts. Dark, unspeakable, evil thoughts. Trying to evaluate my thoughts was exhausting. "Why am I thinking this way? That's not true." It was a constant barrage of lies and demonic attacks that battled to destroy me.

Believing they were my own thoughts, I'd confess them to the Lord over and over again. *I must have committed the unpardonable sin*, I thought. God has turned against me. Feeling like God's finger of judgment was on me was the most

3

devastating part of my depression. The one relationship I held most dear seemed to have disappeared.

I started reexamining my soul. Were there any past sins that I had committed and hadn't taken care of? Was God angry with me for that? I thought of an instance when I had invited all my neighbors to a Bible study at my home. I put the invitations in their mailboxes. Tampering with someone's mailbox is a crime. *That must be it*, I thought. I went around and apologized to my neighbors for that intrusion. There was no relief.

There must be more sin, I thought. There had been a time during a Bible study that I shared something I had done. Maybe I had done that out of a proud heart. Maybe I had a problem with pride. *Yes, that must be it*, I thought. Calling up the table leader of the Bible study, I confessed that I had shared my story out of pride. She was very gracious and said that the story had encouraged her. I was thankful she was so kind, but there was no relief.

I searched my heart, going back even farther. Seven years earlier, I had been out with a group of friends at a local pie shop. A good friend from church came over and sat down with us awhile. I moved over so she could share the booth with us, but my attitude was rotten. I didn't say anything, but I knew the attitude was wrong. I drove to her place of work and apologized for the bad attitude I had had seven years earlier. She did not remember, but was very gracious and loving. I was thankful she was kind, but there was no relief.

I drove to a parking lot and just sat there in my car. I thought, *On the way home, I will die in a car accident.* I had a very real sense of impending doom. I had tried my best to ask everyone to forgive me, but the huge weight of guilt would not budge.

The national elections were coming up. Robert and I enjoyed sitting down each evening and watching the political pundits duke it out. One evening as I was sitting in front of the TV, I thought I saw hell. I was hallucinating, but at the time I thought God was showing me where I was going. I was terrified and had no insight on how to process any of this.

On election night, as the polls started to close, I went to bed. "Where are you going?" asked my husband.

"To bed," I replied. I didn't care who won; it didn't matter.

In November, things really started to go south. Robert and I were watching a movie one evening. There was a scene where an older man was giving instructions to a young boy. "I'm not the right one for the job. I can't do it," said the boy.

The old man replied, "You are exactly the one I want. I want you to do the job."

In my illness, I sometimes felt that I was living the scenes I saw on television. Sometimes the characters seemed to be talking to me. I felt that way that night. I heard that conversation and believed that it was for me. I still believe God used that scene to encourage me when my mind was not working. Yes, He knew where I was. Yes, he had chosen the right person to go through this. Strangely, I felt comforted.

By this time, I thought I knew what was wrong with me. I must have had a stroke. Along with my mental changes, my fingers would curl up, my fine motor skills weren't working correctly, and my hands felt like dog paws. My speech was slurred and I couldn't think. But no one believed me.

My husband suggested I call my obstetrician. I reached out to him, and he referred me to a psychiatric office that week.

When the day of the office visit came, my husband and I went together. We told the doctor all my strange symptoms. He sat there calmly and said, "You have depression."

I balked! *Depression is when you aren't thankful or happy,* I thought. My mind was reeling from his diagnosis. It felt like a slap in the face. He wasn't taking me seriously; he must not be understanding the gravity of my condition.

He went on to explain about neurons and hormones and other things. He lost me at *depression,* but my engineering husband listened to all the details. They seemed to make perfect sense to him. I got a prescription for an antidepressant that was supposed to give me some more energy and made an appointment to come back in four weeks.

I left the doctor's office angry. *He totally blew me off,* I thought. I couldn't fathom that all my catastrophic, life-altering symptoms could come from depression. This was something way more serious. *Depression is a spiritual issue,* I thought. I rejected the diagnosis and did not take the medicine.

I went home and thought, *I feel so far from God. Am I going to find Him by taking an antidepressant? Is God in the bottle? Can I get right with God by taking a pill? That doesn't make sense. I'm not going to take it. There must be another explanation.*

The next morning I met with one of my lifelong friends at my favorite coffee shop. I don't even know how I drove there, because I was having trouble staying alert to my surroundings. I felt like I was in some sort of dream world, that I was just an observer of everything that was going on around me. Right away she noticed something was wrong. I told her what my symptoms were, that I thought I'd had a stroke, and that no one would take me to the hospital. I was slurring my speech and had a hard time staying awake. She drove me straight home and told my husband that she had never seen me like this before.

My husband called my mom, who was hosting a wedding at the church. She left quickly and came right over. All dressed up, she walked into my house and said, "Go upstairs and get in your pajamas." My husband and my mom convinced me to take the medicine that the doctor had given me. I reluctantly took my first antidepressant, with a hope for recovery. It was just the beginning of a nightmare.

That afternoon, I read all the information I could find on the prescription that the doctor had given me. I read about how it worked and about all of the side effects. One side effect I noticed was the potential triggering of a "fight or flight" response from the release of adrenaline into the bloodstream. After reading extensively about this drug, I thought it might just be what I needed.

That evening, I stood at the front screen door, enjoying the cool breeze as it floated in. My husband was working outside and the kids were watching a cartoon in the living room. All of a sudden I became very irritable. Things were becoming crystal clear. Suddenly, I was in a heightened state of alertness. With wolf-like senses, I turned to look at my children as they were playing and making noise in front of the cartoons. I felt like a predator, and they were the prey. I called out to my husband, *"Robert!"*

Like an arrow that shot through my brain, I had the thought that my predatory urge was a reaction to the medicine, that I was having a fight or flight response. A command came to me, "Go take this out on your furniture." I ran downstairs to the den. A strength I didn't know I had and a fury that was not my own surged through me, and I vented its violence on the couch and the floor. Robert was with me as I crawled around on my hands and knees, punching the floor and screaming, "What's wrong with me?" I threw my head back and pulled my hair. I continued pounding the ground until my rage eased.

The episode ended and my husband and I were exhausted— physically, emotionally, mentally. How much more could we take? I went to bed upset. The very pill that was supposed to help me had turned out to be a nightmare. As I fell asleep, I was unaware that the nightmare was not over.

Around two in the morning, I woke up out of a sound sleep. I started to feel agitated. *Oh no!* I thought. *It's happening again!* I went down to the basement without waking my husband. I called my dad on the phone. In a shaky voice I told him, "Dad, I'm not doing good and I'm afraid of what I might do."

He said, "I'm coming over," and hung up the phone.

We had a large treadmill stored in the corner of the basement. I aggressively yanked it over to an outlet and plugged it in. In a rage, I put on my running shoes. Wearing my nightgown and robe, I got on the treadmill and pressed the incline button again and again. I began pounding out my aggression.

Robert came down into the basement. "Your dad called," he said with a bewildered look on his face. I just kept climbing the steep slope until the tsunami of negative energy subsided.

When my dad arrived, he came downstairs and saw that I was a wreck. "I'm going crazy," I told him.

He prayed with me and tried to comfort me. "You're not going crazy," he said.

I was not convinced. The pill was an extended release tablet, so I knew that in another six hours I was likely to experience another episode.

That morning was a Sunday, and I encouraged Robert to go to church. He had seen enough and needed to get out of the house. I called my sister Leah and asked if she would come over to watch me for the morning. We were in my bedroom, and I was lying in bed when my nose started to bleed. I began crying and said, "My brain is bleeding. I've had a stroke and no one believes me." Through my sobs I could see she didn't know what to say. I was falling apart. Everyone said I had depression. When I took the medicine I was supposed to take, I turned into an animal. And I was afraid. I was afraid it would happen again, soon.

My husband and I had told her what had happened earlier. "If I start getting really aggressive, go lock yourself in the other bedroom with the baby and do not open the door!" I said. Thankfully, that episode never happened.

I called the doctor that afternoon. "That medicine has way too much energy!" I told him angrily. He told me he would switch me to a different type of antidepressant, one that was milder and had fewer side effects.

Scared to death to try another medicine, I decided it would be best to experiment with this one away from my family. I asked my parents if I could stay at their house while I took the first dose of this new pill.

That night my brain felt like it was bound in a tourniquet and that blood was oozing out, increasing the pressure in my skull. In the middle of the night I poked my head into my parents' room. My mom shot up. Remembering the description of what had happened after I took my first antidepressant, she was concerned about what this new antidepressant might do. "What's the matter?" she asked.

"My head hurts so bad, I think I'm having a stroke."

My mom got up, and walked me back to my room. "You're not having a stroke," she said and then told me to get in bed. She crawled in next to me and rubbed my back to help me relax. Rest was elusive for me.

The doctor gave me Xanax for my headaches and told me I could take one every six hours. It only helped for half that time. I was still afraid to be left alone. I couldn't focus. I felt like God was against me. I was constantly evaluating my bizarre state of mind, and it was wearing me out.

I felt totally detached from reality, like life was just a TV episode and didn't connect to me in any way. I'd look at Robert and think, "Who are you?" I didn't have normal emotions anymore. I felt flat and distant. The person in the mirror looked familiar but inside she had disappeared.

Between my feelings of judgment, guilt, and detachment, my mind was a constant battle zone. My headaches only got worse as I tried to figure it all out. As much as I felt like I was in another world, I remember clinging to Robert and asking him to pray aloud for me. I needed to hear him pray. Nothing could penetrate this detached state I was in, but somehow when I heard him pray, it comforted me. It was strangely familiar. I clung to his faith.

I found a verse that I'd say over and over to myself out loud when I was really struggling. It was Psalm 46:1: "God is our refuge and strength, an ever present help in trouble." I'd say, "You are an ever present help in trouble, and I am in trouble!"

Robert needed help. His mom came in for two weeks and gave him a hand with the house. He had the pressures of a young family, a sick wife, and his business. He didn't understand what was going on with me or if I would ever get better. We were devastated.

This was a very private struggle for me and my husband. My family and close friends knew. I didn't want anybody else to know because I was embarrassed about what they might think. I used to believe that people who took antidepressants were just trying to mask their real spiritual problems. I thought they were unwilling to deal with the main issues they were struggling with, and used medicine to make them feel better. But now, I was the one with depression. The view from in here looked so different than it had from the outside. The passing judgments I'd dished out now made me cringe. I knew the opinion I used to have, and I didn't want people thinking that about me.

When you go through something terrible like this, people who have suffered in the same way are more willing to share their stories. I was shocked by what I found out. There are a lot of Christians who are struggling with depression. They were covertly walking around at church. I felt like I was standing all alone, then opened the closet door and found a bunch of people in the same situation I was in.

I was shocked but quickly understood why they preferred to remain quiet. It was because of people like me, who chalked off people with depression as not spiritual enough to handle their problems. This was a painful realization.

I began to feel that Christians were hypocrites. The prayer list was only for people with acceptable illnesses; that there was a whole group of us who were suffering in silence out of fear of being judged. This was how I perceived things. I had denied my own diagnosis because it didn't fit into the mold I had for depression. I was struggling to reconcile the fact that I could have a mental illness with my previous opinion of depression. It was too much to process.

God was so faithful to me when I was in this dark pit. I had no idea where I was or what I was fighting, but thanks be to God, He did! I was never out of His sight. Even though I felt He was against me, He was actually carrying and defending me. Job 16:19–21 says, "Even now my witness is in heaven; my advocate is on high. My intercessor is my friend as my eyes pour out tears to God; on behalf of a man he pleads with God as a man pleads for his friend."

My mind was not working, and I didn't trust it. But God visibly encouraged me throughout my ordeal. I can look back and see that through all the dark notes of my depression, He orchestrated for me a visual melody of His love.

My dad told me that he was going to give me some pocket money every week for a whole year. "Are you serious?" I said. He was. Starting that November, every week he gave me some "fun money."

At first, I used the money to get massages, relieving my headaches and all the tension that had built up in my body. After a while, I used it on treats like getting my nails done. I looked forward to those little highlights each week. They became my therapy.

A group of my close friends from church surprised me with a box full of my favorite things: coffee, chocolate, a gift card for a massage, a candle. They just wanted me to know they cared. God was showing me in practical ways His love for me, and I remember them like landmarks. He was there.

There was another week that the Lord showed His love to me through my mailbox. Every time the mail was delivered, I got a surprise. One day I won a coffee maker from my eye doctor. Another day I got a beautiful gift from a dear friend. I remember thinking, "Lord, what will it be today?"

My mom came over every week and watched the kids so I could grocery shop alone. One day, I came home and my mom had a look of disbelief on her face. "You will not believe what just happened!" she said. A friend from church had dropped off a week's worth of meals that she had made for me, along with a bunch of snacks and a gift. That was such a boost of encouragement. I was blown away. I was so thankful for her. Since my mind was not working, God was visibly showing me that He loved me, and that He was there.

I was not getting better. Sometimes I shared my thoughts with my mom or my husband, just to let them know what I was dealing with. Even my best attempts at rational thought completely betrayed me. My brain, no matter how hard I tried to think and process information, didn't work. What I saw, felt, and thought did not match up to what a healthy mind saw, felt, and thought. You cannot talk sense into someone with depression, no matter how logical your argument is.

When a Christian becomes ill, they may not feel God's presence, but He is there. He is present with His children whether they are healthy or sick. He fights for them. He guides them. He protects them. He is there when other Christians tell them that their struggles are spiritual and they don't need medicine. He is there when they leave the doctor's office crying because they feel like spiritual failures. He works through His saints to comfort them. He works around other saints who would hurt and discourage them.

Hebrews 4:15 says, "We do not have a high priest who is unable to sympathize with our weakness, but we have one who has been tempted in every way, just as we are—yet was without sin." I wonder if Jesus experienced physical depression when he was in the wilderness. He fasted for forty days and nights.

How would your body and mind be affected with no food for well over a month? I praise God that he does not leave us in our battles alone. In 2 Peter 2:9, the Bible says, "If this is so, then the Lord knows how to rescue godly men from trials."

My recovery was slow. Battling constant fatigue, I focused on my primary responsibilities: my husband, my kids, my home. I didn't have the energy to do anything extra. I was asked to help out in different ministries. I didn't trust myself to commit to anything. I knew my fatigue would overrule my commitment. Simple tasks like going to the store wore me out. Staying home was about all I could manage, and I spent a lot of that time on the couch. I didn't trust myself to drive very far. I knew I couldn't stay focused for long periods of time.

About seven months after I started the new medicine, I was driving the kids home from vacation Bible school. We lived a half-hour drive from church. I was on the interstate, and it began to rain. The water seemed to pour out of the sky in sheets. My windshield wipers couldn't keep up. It seemed I was surrounded by a cloud, with the steady sound of pounding rain hitting the top of the van. I started to feel sleepy and struggled to keep my eyelids open. There were no other mental stimuli, no landmarks or buildings, just the lulling sound of the rain and the white windshield. I felt like I was disengaging from my environment.

Panicking, I knew I had to stay alert. I bit my tongue as hard as I could, then my cheek. Over and over I tried to keep awake by applying pain. I slapped my legs, then my face. I felt like it was just a dream, but I knew I was on the interstate going around fifty miles an hour, trucks flying by me. I tried to stay in touch with my environment, thinking, "Please, Lord, get me home."

By the time I finally pulled into my driveway, I was exhausted. That episode frightened me, and after that, I refused to drive long distances.

It took about two years to start feeling like myself again. My mind stopped harassing me, but I struggled with fatigue for a long time. What I experienced was major depressive disorder with psychotic features. Phychosis is "a severe mental disorder of organic and/ or emotional origin, marked by impairment of the ability to think, communicate, respond emotionally, and interpret reality; the person is unable to meet the ordinary demands of life and frequently undergoes regressive behavior, delusions, and hallucinations." [1] A delusion is, "a false belief maintained even against contradictory evidence or logical argument." [2] A hallucination is defined as a, "perception of objects or events that do not exist." [3]

When I thought my baby was laughing at me, it was a delusion. When I took that first medication, though my mind was very ill, God worked though my sick mind and commanded me to the safety of my den, to vent my adrenaline surge on the floor.

I never felt like swinging from the chandeliers, never felt a glowing blissfulness in the midst of my problems. That is what I used to think people experienced when they took antidepressants. Instead I was tired. I lost my spunk and felt emotionally flat. The scope of my activities decreased.

My goal was to get off all my medicine and move past those nightmarish two years. I tried to wean off the medication a couple times, but each time the symptoms would come back after twelve weeks. "This time will be different," I'd tell myself, and I'd try again. I searched for natural products that would help. I tried exercise. No matter what I tried adding to my regimen, I was never able to wean off my medicine.

At this point, I knew that my depression was not a spiritual problem, but I still wanted to know why. Why did I get it? Something must have caused it. I went to different doctors in search of an answer. In the back of my mind, I still thought that I might have had a stroke, and that maybe that's what caused the depression.

I had test after test. They checked my thyroid, my cortisol and vitamin levels. I was tested for Lyme's disease, had an EEG and an ACTH stimulation test. They did an MRI of the brain, on which I had two second opinions. Everything was normal. There would be no answers.

During those two years, I learned how hard it was to endure life with this illness. It was physically, emotionally, mentally, and spiritually draining. No one really understood what I had gone through. I could not understand it myself. What I did know, however, was that I was getting better, and that gave me strength to go on.

CHAPTER TWO

ROUND TWO

Three years after Matthew was born, the Lord gave us a girl! When I found out I was pregnant, I stopped one of the two medicines that I was on. After I delivered, I restarted the second medicine. The antidepressants had kept me safely above water. I did, however, continue to experience extreme fatigue, both mentally and physically. I assumed these symptoms came from the side effects of my medication, and accepted them, also allowing for the fact that any mother of four would naturally be tired mentally and physically. I fought constant fatigue as I cared for my family for the next five years.

In June 2012, our family moved from Illinois to Virginia. My husband, being from Virginia, had for several years expressed a desire to move back down South. I was content living in Illinois near my family, and had resisted his preference for many years. I decided to ask the Lord to lead me in this area. I prayed, if it was the Lord's will that we move, for the Lord to change my heart and make me willing. My desire was to stay, but I did not want to get in the way of what God wanted for my family.

My adamant refusals to move slowly changed to a surrender of my will—a surrender from "me first" to "God, You lead." Even though my heart was changing, it was too difficult for me to verbalize. I knew that the Lord was melting my will to conform to His will, but I didn't want to tell my husband. I knew that once I told him, I would be ripped away from my family.

The Lord brought about the conversation, and we began the process of moving. For the next four months, as we packed and planned, I grieved deeply over this move. All through the process, I focused on the children. I wanted this to be a positive experience for them.

We moved in June and hit the ground running. I joined a pool before we arrived at our new house, so we would have somewhere to go. The first church we tried in our area was a good fit for us, and that was a blessing. We went to the library and the lake, explored the area, and searched for the best doughnut shops. The kids adjusted well.

I, however, felt like I wasn't doing so well. The stress of moving and the emotional turmoil I had gone through had affected me physically and mentally. I searched on my computer for a local doctor. At my first appointment, I gave him my history. I told him I felt like I was beginning to slip back into depression. I was having trouble thinking, I had difficulty getting out of bed, nothing was enjoyable anymore, and everything seemed to overwhelm me.

He told me that one of the medications I had been taking for the past eight years had become ineffective, and that he would replace it with a new antidepressant. He told me that this new medicine should also give me more energy.

I was excited to try it. I had struggled with fatigue for so long that I hadn't considered I could live life without it. I started the medicine with great hopes, but as soon as I took it, I became very irritable. This new antidepressant made me angry, like I had pepper under my skin. I waited until my next appointment and told the doctor how I felt. He told me to stop my other old medication as well, and only take the antidepressant that he had given me.

I slowly began to spiral downward. My legs felt like they weighed a thousand pounds each. Just to walk from the bed to the bathroom was an extremely difficult task. I had to get up early, wake up all four of our children, feed them, and get them off to school. This was a daunting task, and I could barely manage it. It made me angry to see how easy it was for my husband to get up, get a cup of coffee, and enjoy his morning. It was effortless for him. I had to climb Mt. Everest every morning; he just had to stop by Starbucks. It seemed so unfair!

Life became miserable for me. It was more than I could handle. I knew what physical depression was this time, but that didn't make it easier to bear. The overwhelming emotional distress isn't any easier to manage just because you know that it is caused by an illness. Knowing it wasn't a sin issue, however, meant I didn't have to carry the additional burden of false guilt.

I would get disproportionately upset over seemingly insignificant comments or actions. I couldn't think, so helping with math homework was an impossible task. Asking me to go to the grocery store was like asking me to shop for and unload ten freight cars' worth of weight. I felt weak at the very thought. My limbs felt like they were tree trunks. They were heavy to move. At times when I walked, my legs would just stop moving, as if the messages from my brain weren't getting to my legs. I had to stop and think, "I am walking, legs. Move!"

Conflict arose in our home from the lack of tools to communicate how I was feeling. It is difficult because the words we use in everyday language—*tired, frustrated, stressed, overwhelmed*—cannot communicate the way a depressed person experiences being tired, frustrated, stressed, or overwhelmed. For the depressed person, these normal feelings are magnified by a hundred.

My husband knew the doctor was changing around my medicine, but he didn't really know how I felt. I was angry all the time, and I felt that my body had become difficult to maneuver. There were times I thought I needed to call an ambulance because I could barely breathe, like my chest was being crushed. My doctor was not responsive to my cries for help. He told me I needed to wait for the medicine to get to a therapeutic level in my body. I knew I was in trouble and had no one to turn to for help.

At Thanksgiving time, I flew home for a few days. My family was aware of my difficulties, and the day I arrived, I had an appointment with my previous doctor. I told him how awful I was feeling and what I was currently taking. He put me back on one of the medicines I had stopped. I began to notice a slight improvement within a few days.

When I returned to Virginia, my new doctor put me back on my original regimen. There were still hiccups in my treatment, however, and after six months I decided to change doctors. I went to see my family practice doctor and gave him my history with depression. He decided to increase the dose of one of the two medicines I had been on for eight years. I was happy with that decision and started taking the adjusted dose, just as he ordered.

Slowly, I noticed that my energy level was improving. I would wake up without feeling like my body was weighted down. I was alert in the morning. I could function without a daily nap.

As I improved, I realized I had suffered from mental and physical fatigue for the previous eight years, not as a side effect from a needed medication, but as a consequence of not being on the right dose of that medication. All I needed was 150 more milligrams, and my body could function without debilitating fatigue.

Those years of my life had been very difficult. I know I am not alone in what I suffer and that there are many untold stories of depression. The Lord allowed me to suffer through this illness for His perfect purposes. Looking back, I see His hand all through my story. There is no doubt He intended the flame to get as hot as it did, for with that intense heat He was able to mold and change me.

I wanted to share with you my private struggle with depression because I had been wrong. I had assumed all depression stemmed from spiritual problems. I was prejudiced against antidepressants and had even judged people I knew for being on them.

While there are many contributing factors to depression in general, we in the church need to realize that we cannot conclude that all depression is spiritual. This prejudice in my own heart added to the burden of my depression and hindered my road to recovery, putting my health and the health of my family at risk. It was this prejudice that choked off the support I could have received from the numerous Christians who also have suffered with major depression. It was this prejudice that isolated me from the power of a praying church that could have been lifting me up. It was this prejudice that the Devil used to make my difficult journey an impossible one.

But it was my Jesus who watched over me and rescued me during my darkest moments. Jesus said, "With man this is impossible, but with God all things are possible" (Matthew 19:26).

CHAPTER THREE

CLOAK, CRIPPLE, CONFUSE

A friend of mine is married to a high school football coach. His team went to the state championship in the fall of 2012. The night before the game, while the players were at home, Coach was at the high school late into the night, studying tapes of their opponent. He wanted to learn their plays and strategies. Learning their strengths and their weaknesses would help him form a better offense and defense. Coach was committed to winning. He did not underestimate his opponent.

We too have an opponent who has a strategy to defeat us. He's been working on his strategy for thousands of years. In 2 Corinthians 2:5–11, Paul encourages the church to forgive a repentant brother and to comfort him, "in order that Satan might not outwit us. For we are not unaware of his schemes."

What I learned during my battle with depression is that our adversary is malicious, evil, and dangerous. His intention is not simply to harm. John 10:10 says, "The thief comes only to steal and kill and destroy."

Our nation spends billions of dollars on weapons of war. We value stealth in the military because the unseen combatant has the advantage. We train teams to go covertly into enemy territory. Being undetected has huge advantages. When the enemy is invisible, you can't see the hit coming.

When we believe that all depression is spiritual and become physically depressed, we do not realize what battle we are fighting. We are at a huge disadvantage. Satan has used this to cause devastation in many families, and we need to become aware of his schemes. We need to understand the battle and understand the tactics our opponent uses on us.

Genesis 2:15–17 says, "The LORD God took the man and put him in the garden of Eden to work it and take care of it. And the LORD God commanded the man, 'You are free to eat from any tree in the garden; but you must not eat from the tree of the knowledge of good and evil, for when you eat of it you will surely die.'"

Genesis 3:1–7 says:

> Now the serpent was more crafty than any of the wild animals the LORD God had made. He said to the woman, "Did God really say, 'You must not eat from any tree in the garden?'"
>
> The woman said to the serpent, "We may eat fruit from the trees in the garden, but God did

say, 'You must not eat fruit from the tree that is in the middle of the garden, and you must not touch it, or you will die.'"

"You will not surely die," the serpent said to the woman. "For God knows that when you eat of it your eyes will be opened and you will be like God, knowing good and evil."

When the woman saw that the fruit of the tree was good for food and pleasing to the eye, and also desirable for gaining wisdom, she took some and ate it. She also gave some to her husband, who was with her, and he ate it. Then the eyes of both of them were opened, and they realized they were naked; so they sewed fig leaves together and made coverings for themselves.

Satan is the Father of Lies. He is the Deceiver. He cast doubt with the question, "Did God really say?" Then he lied and told Eve that God would not do what God said He would do. Satan lied again and told her she would be like God. He appealed to her vanity.

Satan works the same way today. When he deceives us into believing that all depression is spiritual, he effectively cloaks the physically depressed person's pathway to recovery. This cripples the ill person in his fight. Satan lies to us and tells us it's our fault. Because we don't know any better, we assist him in judging ourselves of wrongdoing. In our vanity, we do not send out a cry for help because that would mean we aren't spiritual. By shrouding the topic of depression in confusion, Satan paralyzes the depressed Christian.

In 1 Peter 5:8, the Bible says, "Be self-controlled and alert. Your enemy the devil prowls around like a roaring lion looking for someone to devour." We, as Christians, need to be alert to the issue of physical depression. We need to pay close attention so we can anticipate the schemes of our adversary and be ready to come to the aid of those who are suffering.

When people are severely depressed, their thought processes slow down. It is difficult to string thoughts together. Satan takes this opportunity to drop lies into their sluggish minds, and they think about those lies over and over. In their illness, they have a difficult time focusing, so they really strain to understand why they are thinking this way. In the process, they dwell on Satan's lies and even assume that they themselves are the source of these thoughts. Their consciences feel unclean, which only adds to their guilt.

In 1 Timothy 2:19, the Bible tells us to fight the good fight by "holding on to faith and a good conscience." When depressed people reject the fact that physical depression exists, they believe that the lies Satan drops into their minds are their own thoughts. They feel their consciences have been defiled.

Our nation as a whole is at the beginning of the mental illness learning curve. Depression is widely misunderstood. We form our opinions from the bits and pieces of information we hear. Our opinions remain unchallenged in the absence of education. It is difficult to accept that a normal, healthy person can, all of a sudden, become depressed. What happens? Does a brain just stop working?

Our organs can malfunction. In 2 Corinthians 4:16, the Bible says, "Therefore we do not lose heart. Though outwardly we are wasting away, yet inwardly we are being renewed day by day." In 1 Corinthians 15:53, the Bible says, "For the perishable must clothe itself with the imperishable, and the mortal with immortality." Our bodies are wasting away; they are mortal and they malfunction. It is the result of the fall.

I have a friend whose daughter developed juvenile diabetes. At first, these friends thought their daughter was simply defying them. She was difficult to manage. She needed more discipline. Then they took her to the doctor and discovered that what she needed was insulin. Her pancreas had stopped functioning correctly and she needed to take insulin to bring her blood sugar levels down. It was the increased blood sugar that had affected her behavior.

That was a very difficult time for the whole family. There was a major learning curve. They had to record everything she ate. They had to learn how to take her blood sugar, how to give insulin, and how to change their eating habits. A whole new world, about which they'd never given a second thought, suddenly became their world.

Depression is just another way that the brain can malfunction. The body gets tired easily; even simple tasks seem difficult. There is irritability, frustration, memory loss, and difficulty concentrating, among other things.

There are different forms of depression, according to the National Institute of Mental Health (NIMH). These include major depression, persistent depressive disorder, psychotic depression, postpartum depression, seasonal affective disorder, and bipolar disorder. [4]

Before I developed major depression, my brain functioned normally. It worked well, so well that I never paid attention to it as an organ. I never considered how fortunate I was to be blessed with a healthy brain. My underappreciated brain worked fast and accurately; it took no effort on my part. This line illustrates a normally functioning brain.

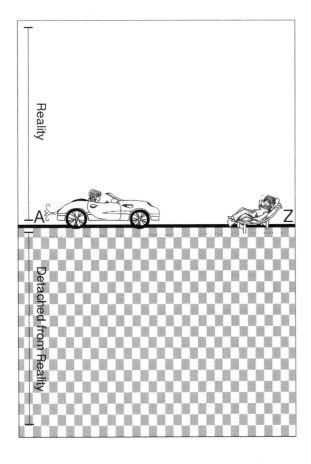

When I became depressed, it was as if my brain had slowed down. I had difficulty concentrating. I couldn't focus, and I physically began to slow down as well.

Depression is a physical illness that affects the brain and the body. Each year about 6.7% of U.S. adults experience major depressive disorder.[1] According to the National Institute of Mental Health, "Major depressive disorder is one of the most common mental disorders in the United States. Women are

70% more likely than men to experience depression during their lifetime." [5]

What I experienced was major depression with psychotic features in the postpartum period, or after the birth of my third child. According to NIMH, "Major depression is characterized by a combination of symptoms that interfere with a person's ability to work, sleep, study, eat and enjoy once-pleasurable activities. Major depression is disabling and prevents a person from functioning normally." [6]

Psychotic depression, as defined by the NIMH, "occurs when a person has severe depression plus some form of psychosis such as having disturbing false beliefs or a break with reality (delusions), or hearing or seeing upsetting things that others cannot hear or see (hallucinations)." [7]

In the Christian community, we use the word *depression* as a catchall phrase that includes spiritual discouragement. When our sweet, trusting, resting fellowship is broken, or when we are wrestling through difficult circumstances and have not surrendered completely to God's will, we will not experience the peace that passes all understanding or the joy we find in God's presence. This causes us to suffer in many ways.

Spiritual discouragement can be caused willfully or ignorantly by worry, resentment, burnout in ministry, fear, sin, disobeying God's Word, unresolved bitterness and anger, or having idols in our lives, just to name a few. It can be caused by not thinking rightly, not trusting God, or not submitting to God's will.

When we grieve the Holy Spirit, there is a break in the fellowship we have with the Holy Spirit. That causes us to become discouraged, overwhelmed, frustrated, and discontent. We feel hopeless and have difficulty making decisions when our souls are in turmoil. We are inwardly at war, our wills against God's will. This disrupts our attitudes and our relationships and saps us of our strength.

A believer with spiritual discouragement can be restored to the sweet, trusting, resting fellowship by repentance, right thinking according to God's Word, and submitting to God's will. The believer can have peace even in a difficult circumstance.

"While the Bible is truly sufficient for everything in the spiritual realm, it doesn't address all the issues in the physical sphere. Thus, appropriate medical or psychiatric care may be God's means of remedying a physical problem." [8] When we express the idea that all depression is spiritual, we put people who have the physical illness of depression at risk by placing obstacles in their pathway to recovery.

According to Christian psychiatrist Dr. Dwight L. Carlson, contemporary life stress can trigger depression in susceptible individuals. [9] This suggests to me that it is possible for the stress of spiritual discouragement to contribute to depression. There are many examples of people in the Bible who experienced stressful periods of spiritual discouragement that led to depression. Among them are David, Job, and Elijah.

There are, however, many physical influences that can contribute to depression, such as nutritional deficiencies, chemical agents, hormone changes, endocrine changes, lack of light, genetic factors, and certain medications. [10] According to NIMH, "Most likely, depression is caused by a combination of genetic, biological, environmental, and psychological factors. Other depressive episodes may occur with or without an obvious trigger." [11]

We need to be careful of our vernacular. When we say *depression*, what do we really mean? Do we mean spiritual discouragement? Are we talking about the normal emotional ups and downs of wrestling through life? Do we understand what the physical illness of major depression is? I had all the classic symptoms of major depression, but neither I nor those around me knew that an illness could present symptoms in this way. I thought that I had done something wrong. Trying to fix my predicament by reading the Bible, praying, and confessing my sin led to exhaustion but not to relief in my spirit. I spent those months after my son was born battling the idea that God was very angry at me.

Jesus knew how I felt. I thought He was mad at me at that time, but He wasn't. I clung to God's Word in Ephesians 6:13: "Therefore put on the full armor of God, so that when the day of evil comes, you may be able to stand your ground, and after you have done everything, to stand." That day of evil had come upon me. Ignorant that I was physically ill, I didn't do everything I could have, but I did everything I knew to do at that time.

The command at the end of that verse is "to stand." This was a comfort because, for me, it was a command just to endure. This was a command not to quit. When I was exhausted and couldn't do anything else, I could do that. I could live through another day. That might not seem significant to some, but to those who have suffered, along with their families, that is an accomplishment. It was a goal, a job. In faith, believing that is what God wanted me to do, I could stand.

How Firm a Foundation
by John Rippon, 1787

How firm a foundation, ye saints of the Lord,
Is laid for your faith in His excellent Word!
What more can He say than to you He hath said,
To you who for refuge to Jesus have fled?

Fear not, I am with thee, O be not dismayed,
For I am thy God, and will still give thee aid;
I'll strengthen thee, help thee, and cause thee to stand,
Upheld by My righteous, omnipotent hand.

When through fiery trials thy pathway shall lie,
My grace, all sufficient, shall be thy supply;
The flame shall not hurt thee; I only design
Thy dross to consume and thy gold to refine.

The soul that on Jesus hath leaned for repose,
I will not, I will not desert to its foes;
That soul, though all hell should endeavor to shake,
I'll never, no, never, no, never forsake!

CHAPTER FOUR

BRAIN VS. BIBLE

For the Christian, the Bible is God's instruction book for life. In 2 Timothy 3:16, the Bible says, "All Scripture is God-breathed and is useful for teaching, rebuking, correcting and training in righteousness." It is the source of all truth. It is our hope, peace, and joy. We find strength from the Bible, God's Word, and are able to find rest and peace in difficult times. When someone is severely depressed, his or her normal thinking pattern is interrupted and emotions are commandeered. When this happens, there is a great disparity between what the brain is telling the person is true and what the Bible tells us is true. This is where the battle rages.

My depressed brain and body had battled to reconcile these two. The more I tried, the more frustrated I became. I felt like a spiritual failure. I had always been able to come to God in the past. If I felt guilty, I would ask Him to show me the error of my ways. I would confess my sin and try to go back and amend my error. He was always faithful to forgive me. I moved on with a clean heart. Having a clear conscience was an utmost priority in my life.

This time, it was different. I tried over and over again; in fact, I wore myself out examining my heart and confessing. I felt guilty about everything. I lived under the sense of inescapable judgment. I tried getting my tired body up earlier than usual to spend more time reading my Bible and focusing on God's Word. It was impossible for me to focus, but I tried and tried. I talked to my parents about my bizarre thinking. They quoted all the right Scriptures, but they couldn't explain how, after I had done all the confessing, my symptoms remained unchanged. No one could understand, especially me. My mind was my enemy, and I couldn't get away from it. I was trapped in my body.

I fought intrusive, disturbing, evil thoughts. I had never thought this way before. All these thoughts seemed to be aimed at destroying my hope, making me feel that I was against God. I didn't know where these thoughts came from, and I didn't want to offend God, but the thoughts wouldn't stop. Eventually, I concluded that I must have lost my salvation. How could Jesus abide in me while I had all these unspeakable thoughts going on in my mind?

This went on with increasing intensity. I felt hollow and empty. The combination of my thoughts and feelings and how I interpreted them was terrifying. My thoughts and feelings were so intense and real that it was difficult to reconcile my beliefs with my reality. They were at odds with each other.

My thoughts and feelings betrayed all I had ever known. It was as if my perspective on every aspect of my life had been stolen and replaced with thoughts and feelings unfamiliar to me. I felt I was to blame. I beat myself up, adding more guilt to my burden.

I had a very real feeling that my time to die was approaching. I sensed it. I didn't know how ill I was or that I had become delusional. I always felt that the next time I got into a vehicle, it would crash and I would die. I was so positive that I was going to die that I started teaching my children about heaven, so they would know more about it when I was gone. I sat down with my husband and told him I thought I was going to die. I told him my wishes for my family afterward. He didn't know what to think.

When a severely depressed person is out of touch with reality, he or she doesn't know it. My husband and I didn't know what we were dealing with. The feelings were absolutely real; I was totally sincere. I wish I had known that I was ill at that time. It would have been a great comfort to us both to have had my symptoms explained. But I didn't know. I thought it was all my fault.

In his book *The God-Shaped Brain*, Christian psychiatrist Dr. Timothy R. Jennings explains, "When people are depressed, the brain circuitry is out of balance. The DLFPC [dorsolateral prefrontal cortex] activity is below normal, so people with depression are impaired in their ability to concentrate, focus, think clearly, plan, organize, problem solve and manage life stress. The anterior cingulate cortex (ACC) is also underactive in depression, contributing to a sense of emotional distance from others and to difficulty making decisions." [12]

Dr. Jennings further states,

> The orbital and medial frontal cortexes are the parts of the brain that convict of wrong and redirect away from inappropriate behavior. When depressed, these two areas are overactive. This means a depressed person experiences intense feelings of inadequacy, guilt and a sense that everything they are doing is wrong. The amygdala, the brain's alarm, is also overactive in depression, causing a constant sense of fear, apprehension, uneasiness, dread or impending doom. And the pleasure center of the brain, the nucleus accumbens, where all pleasure registers, is unresponsive when depressed. So the depressed person experiences an overwhelming sense of gloom, guilt, inadequacy, fear, apprehension, emotional blunting, distance from others, inability to think clearly, difficulty with problem solving, a sense of being overwhelmed,

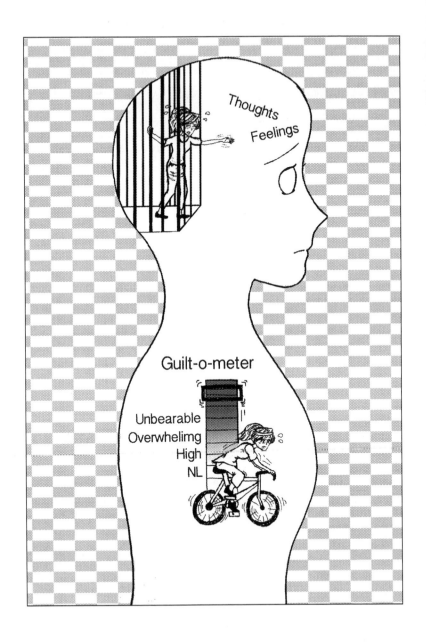

> and impairments in decision making—but no
> pleasure when objectively good events occur. [13]

I wish my husband and I could have sat down with a counselor familiar with this illness, someone who could have explained what was happening in my brain that caused me to feel this way. It was my illness that caused me to feel overwhelming guilt and hindered my ability to think clearly and focus on God's Word. If I had been told, "Yes, the thoughts are disturbing, and the feelings are real, but you have come to the wrong conclusion," then I would have had some comfort.

God does love me. I am saved. Though my hope may feel gone, it is ever present. I had a very serious illness that could be treated. I was experiencing classic symptoms of major depression with psychotic features, and with treatment, I could improve. I wish someone had told me that from the beginning.

Proverbs 4:23 says, "Above all else, guard your heart, for it is the wellspring of life."

And 2 Corinthians 10:5 says, "And we take captive every thought to make it obedient to Christ." These two verses tell us to guard our hearts and make our thoughts obedient to Christ. When you have physical depression, you can't think or focus, and your mind is bombarded with terrible thoughts. It is difficult, if not impossible, to take any thought and address it. The depressed brain gives a person an overwhelming sense of guilt. The depressed person feels that he or she is not keeping and guarding the heart. We usually associate guilt with sin, but in depression, the source of guilt is the physically depressed brain.

My faith had been brutally attacked by this illness, and I was devastated. Jesus had always been the anchor of my soul, but inside I felt detached. Within the context of these vivid thoughts and feelings, nothing in life mattered anymore. It was as though I had been severed from Jesus, my anchor, and that erased all hope.

Because I thought all depression was spiritual, my decision to go to the doctor made me feel as though I was turning to the dark side, as if I was turning from God to the world for help. Receiving the diagnosis of depression made me feel slighted. *How can a pill fix my relationship with God?* I thought.

In the illness of physical depression, Satan sets up his ambush and expertly disarms the believer. Depression is especially effective when its source is concealed, as it was in my case by my lack of education.

For the severely depressed Christian, thinking and emotions are not normal. They are rearranged by the alterations in brain function. Satan uses this opportunity to confuse a believer's emotions, to make the believer doubt God's love, to fill the believer's mind with garbage, and to take away the believer's weapons.

Toward the end of Paul's letter to the Ephesians, he says, "Finally, be strong in the Lord and in his mighty power. Put on the full armor of God so that you can take your stand against the devil's schemes" (Ephesians 6:10–11).

45

That armor of God is available to the believer. Ephesians 6:14–17 says, "Stand firm then, with the belt of truth buckled around your waist, with the breastplate of righteousness in place, and with your feet fitted with the gospel of peace. In addition to all this, take up the shield of faith, with which you can extinguish all the flaming arrows of the evil one. Take the helmet of salvation and the sword of the Spirit, which is the Word of God." I thought I had done that; I thought I had been walking with the Lord. I couldn't figure out how I had become so defenseless.

The first piece of armor is the belt of truth. If you are living your life according to the truth of God's Word, you are ready in case of attack. The illness of depression, however, makes it very difficult to concentrate or focus. You are unable to think, and you are disengaged from your surroundings. You no longer feel ready for anything, and your once truth-focused thoughts turn into confusion.

The breastplate of righteousness is the second piece of armor described for us. This is used to protect our vital organs, especially our hearts. With the illness of depression, however, our thoughts and feelings are distorted. Thinking rightly according to God's Word seems out of reach.

Our confidence that God loves us now begins to waver. Our feet, once ready to go into battle with confidence and peace, now are hesitant, unsure that God is really on our side. With our disturbing thoughts and overwhelming sense of condemnation, we are uncertain where we stand with God. Our confidence has melted into fear.

Before I became ill, I trusted that God was in control. I wanted to live an obedient life. My shield of faith, which was my total trust in God, had extinguished my fears and doubts in the past. Once I became ill, the feeling of condemnation seemed to intensify. *God is angry at me* I thought. *He is no longer guarding my life.* At that point, I had no shield of protection; every arrow hit its mark.

With my helmet of salvation, I had previously felt that no matter how bad life got, I was saved, and one day I would be in heaven with Jesus. This was a great comfort as I went through previous trials. In my illness, however, I doubted my salvation. I felt that God was angry at me and His heavy hand of judgment was on me. My last piece of protection had been removed.

This is the private battle of the physically depressed Christian. With no outside counsel or encouragement, no insight into the truth of what is really going on, no comfort and support from fellow believers, how does one survive? When your thoughts and feelings seem so real and your faith seems obliterated, what conclusion do you draw? What do you believe? This was the very exhausting daily battle that I lived.

What was real? My feelings felt real. What was true? My mind was out of commission. When you have severe depression, you wrestle to reconcile what you know to be true from God's Word with this new reality in which you are now living, tormented in your thoughts and misguided in your emotions. This is why it is so important to be treated medically. But it is also vitally important that the church continues to offer strength and hope to the person in despair.

Satan took my illness and used it to disarm me. All I had left was the sword of the Spirit, the Word of God. Jesus is the Word of God. The medical treatment eventually began to alleviate my horrible symptoms, but it was Jesus I credit with carrying me throughout the illness, protecting me, fighting for me, providing for me, defending me, and mending me. It was Jesus, the Word of God, who was the hero.

CHAPTER FIVE

THE UNPARDONABLE SIN

At a certain point, depression makes you feel completely underwater and there is no way to pull yourself up above the surface. You feel out of touch with reality, like you are living in a foreign world that you never knew existed. Your feelings of condemnation and impending doom are just the ground work the enemy has laid for his next deception: to convince you that you've committed the unpardonable sin and are rejected by God.

What is the unpardonable sin? In the book of Matthew, the Pharisees were saying that Jesus was casting out demons by the power of Beelzebub. The Pharisees were attributing to Beelzebub the miracles that Jesus was performing. Jesus tells them in Matthew 12:31-32, "And so I tell you, every sin and blasphemy will be forgiven men, but the blasphemy against the

Spirit will not be forgiven. Anyone who speaks a word against the Son of Man will be forgiven, but anyone who speaks against the Holy Spirit will not be forgiven, either in this age or in the age to come." He said this because the Pharisees were saying that Jesus had an evil spirit.

Dr. Henry H. Halley explains this passage:

> Though the miracles were entirely benevolent in their nature, yet so hardened and hypocritical were the Pharisees that they attributed them to Satanic origin. Such vile and devilish accusations were evidence of a nature almost beyond redemption. This may be the import of Jesus' words, a condition of heart to which they were perilously near. In Luke 12:10 the unpardonable sin is connected with the denial of Christ. Jesus seems to make a distinction between sin against himself, and sin against the Holy Spirit (32). Quite commonly the Unpardonable Sin is understood thus: rejecting Christ, while as yet he was in the flesh, his work unfinished, when even his disciples did not understand him, was forgivable. But after his work was completed, and the Holy Spirit was come, then, in full knowledge, deliberate final rejection of the Holy Spirit's offer of Christ would constitute the 'eternal sin which hath never forgiveness'. [14]

Dr. G. Campbell Morgan explains this passage this way:

> The sin against the Holy Ghost is the ultimate
> refusal to believe on the testimony of the Spirit
> concerning Jesus Christ. The sin against the
> Holy Ghost is persistent, determined, and final
> rejection of the Spirit's demonstration of the
> meaning of the Kingdom, and of the power of
> the King.
>
> In the final words of the King this statement
> is found; 'Out of the abundance of the heart
> the mouth speaketh.' Notice that principle.
> Speaking against the Holy Ghost does not
> consist in a theory advanced; nor in a sentence
> that drops thoughtlessly from the lips. When a
> man says I will not believe the testimony, he
> does so because in his heart he is refusing the
> King. That is the unpardonable sin. There is no
> sin under heaven that may not be put away by
> infinite mercy, through the Cross, except the sin
> which declines to receive the mercy, to receive
> the grace, because it declines to submit to the
> scepter of the King. [15]

Blasphemy against the Holy Spirit is **not** the same thing
as being attacked by blasphemous thoughts. The former stems
from within the heart of a man who, with full knowledge,
willfully rejects, insults and speaks evil of the Holy Spirit. The

latter is an attack from the enemy in an attempt to cause the believer to doubt God and God's Word, to cause the believer to believe the lie that they have committed blasphemy and to drive them to desperation.

Regarding blasphemous thoughts, nineteenth-century English preacher C.H. Spurgeon said:

> These thoughts, if you hate them, are not yours but are injections of the devil. He is responsible and not you. If you strive against them, they are no more yours than are the cursings and falsehoods of rioters in the street. It is by means of these thoughts that the devil wants to drive you to despair, or at least keep you from trusting Jesus. [16]

I wanted to assign these feeling of judgment and condemnation to a cause, but could not find one. I began to have these bizarre and blasphemous thoughts that would come at the strangest times. They were ugly, disrespectful thoughts that would rattle my entire person. I tried to stop them from coming but it was of no use. I would confess these thoughts over and over, but was unable to control them. I was my harshest critic, and found myself wondering if I had committed the unpardonable sin. My thinking was so fuzzy, I had become so confused.

Why am I thinking this way? I was horrified by my thoughts and began to feel as though I was possessed. *Can a Christian be possessed? Can Christ live in me if I am having these awful, blasphemous thoughts?* I could not verbalize these thoughts aloud they were so heinous in nature. I was completely desperate for an explanation, for without one I was driven to my own conclusion. I had committed the unpardonable sin, blasphemy.

Spurgeon states:

> I have heard another say, 'I am tormented with horrible thoughts. Wherever I go, blasphemies steal in on me. Frequently at my work a dreadful suggestion forces itself upon me. Even in my bed I am startled from my sleep by whispers of the evil one. I cannot get away from this horrible temptation.' Friend, I know what you mean, for I myself have been hunted by this wolf. A man might as well hope to fight a swarm of flies with a sword as to master his own thoughts when they are set on by the devil. A poor tempted soul, assailed by satanic suggestions, is like a traveler I have read about. His head and ears and whole body were attacked by a swarm of angry bees. They stung him everywhere and threatened to kill him. I do not wonder that you feel that you have no strength to stop these hideous and abominable thoughts which Satan pours into your soul. Yet, I would remind you of the Scriptures before us,

'When we were yet without strength, in due
time Christ died for the ungodly'. [17]

Let me lay out two truths. Once you have received Jesus
Christ as your Lord and Savior, you are saved. You cannot lose
your salvation. John 10:28-30 says, "I give them eternal life, and
they shall never perish; no one can snatch them out of my hand.
My Father, who has given them to me, is greater than all; no
one can snatch them out of my Father's hand. I and the Father
are one." Not even you can snatch yourself out of the Father's
hand. God reminds us that Our Father is greater than all, and
that He has us in His hand!

Secondly, this attack against believers is not new. "No
temptation has seized you except what is common to man.
And God is faithful; he will not let you be tempted beyond what
you can bear. But when you are tempted, he will also provide
a way out so that you can stand up under it" (1Corinthians
10:13). This is a common tactic employed by the enemy. Those
who have suffered this, and have shared their experiences, are
a great comfort to others. Their stories help expose this trap
for what it is.

In John Bunyan's book *Grace Abounding to the Chief of
Sinners* he states:

> For, about the space of a month after, a very
> great storm came down upon me, which handled
> me twenty times worse than all I had met with

before; it came stealing upon me, now by one piece, then by another: First, all my comfort was taken from me; then darkness seized upon me; after which, whole floods of blasphemies, both against God, Christ, and the scriptures, were poured upon my spirit, to my great confusion and astonishment. These blasphemous thoughts were such as stirred up questions in me against the very being of God, and of His only beloved Son: As, whether there were in truth, a God or Christ? And whether the holy scriptures were not rather a fable, and cunning story, than the holy and pure word of God? [18]

George Whitefield once preached a sermon on 2 Corinthians 2:11, titled *Satan's Devices.*

But amongst all the devices that Satan makes use of, 'to get an advantage over us,' there is none in which he is more successful, or by which he grieves the children of God worse, than a fourth device I am going to mention: his troubling you with blasphemous, profane, unbelieving thoughts. And sometimes to such a degree, that they are as tormenting as the rack.

Some indeed are apt to impute all such evil thoughts to a disorder of body. But those who know anything of the spiritual life can inform you with greater certainty that, for the generality, they proceed from that wicked one the devil, who, no doubt, has power given him from above, as well now as formerly, to disorder the body, as he did Job's, that he may with the more secrecy and success, work upon, ruffle, and torment the soul. [19]

As Whitefield explains, this deception has two components: the physical component, "to disorder the body" [20] and the spiritual component, so he (the devil) can "work upon, ruffle and torment the soul." [21] As we have discussed earlier, depression can cause feelings of detachment, condemnation and of impending doom. In severe cases it can be accompanied by delusions and hallucinations. In this position the Christian is extremely vulnerable. Confused about the source of his guilt and not able to lift its' burden, the Christian begins to doubt God's love for him. He begins to doubt God's presence. The attack of these blasphemous thoughts causes additional torment. The Christian is bewildered by this and begins to wonder if he is the source of these thoughts.

In John Bunyan's book *The Pilgrim's Progress*, the main character *Christian* is assaulted in a similar way.

One thing I would not let slip. I took notice that now poor Christian was so confounded that he did not know his own voice; and thus

I perceived it. Just when he was come over against the mouth of the burning pit, one of the wicked ones got behind him, and stepped up softly to him, and whisperingly suggested many grievous blasphemies to him, which he verily thought had proceeded from his own mind. This put Christian more to it than anything that he met with before, even to think that he should now blaspheme Him that he loved so much before. Yet if he could have helped it, he would not have done it; but he had not the discretion either to stop his ears, or to know from whence these blasphemies came. [22]

When a physically depressed person's brain is functioning slowly, he is not able to control the thoughts that come into his head. And when those thoughts do come in, he is not able to sort through them. Satan will take advantage of this illness and shoot his flaming, blasphemous arrows into one's mind, and they sit there and rot. The depressed Christian, confused about what the unpardonable sin is, may assume his current condition is a result of having unwittingly committed it. This is Satan's scheme, to make him believe he has been rejected by God and is condemned, so he can use that momentum for his end game. It is so important during this time for the depressed person to be reminded of truth.

I remember a few specific times, when my brain was not functioning, that the words of others were enough for me to cling to. I remember my mom responding to my despair saying that God was with me, that He was in fact covering me. She raised her hands and showed me, like an umbrella. I had no confidence in myself because I didn't trust my thoughts; it was as if my confidence lay on the floor like a clothes hanger. That moment encouraged me and allowed me to pick up that hanger and hook it to her confidence. Another time, I remember telling my mother-in-law that I would never get better. And she looked at me and said, "You are going to get better, I know it." She really believed it, too. I took another hanger off the floor and hung it on her confidence. I remember asking my husband, before he went to work, to please pray for me out loud. Hearing him pray for me allowed me to cling to his faith. When I felt I couldn't go on, that nothing was right, the truth that other people spoke into my life was what I was able to hang onto.

When someone has severe depression, we need to realize that their mind is ill. What they say and feel may not match the person you know them to be. They may have been a very strong person of faith and this behavior and lack of faith is totally uncharacteristic of them. It is because they are ill. They need medical attention and spiritual support. This dragon has two heads and both need to be addressed.

Spurgeon states:

> This evil will also come upon us, we know
> not why, and then it is all the more difficult to
> drive away. Causeless depression is not to be

> reasoned with, nor can David's harp charm it
> away by sweet discoursings. As well fight with
> the mist as with this shapeless, undefinable,
> yet all-beclouding hopelessness. One affords
> himself no pity when in this case, because
> it seems so unreasonable, and even sinful to
> be troubled without manifest cause; and yet
> troubled the man is, even in the very depths of
> his spirit. [23]

You cannot talk someone out of this type of depression for it can cause a person to become illogical. You can, however stand on truth in the midst of their despair, lending your faith as a support. Your unwavering trust in God's faithfulness to his Word may not convince them all is well, but it will be a light unto them.

Ecclesiastes 3:14, "I know that everything God does will endure forever; nothing can be added to it and nothing taken from it. God does it so that men will revere him." When you are saved by the grace of God, it is permanent. You are saved forever; nothing can be added or taken away from your salvation!

Romans 8:38-39, "For I am convinced that neither death nor life, neither angels nor demons, neither the present nor the future, nor any powers, neither height nor depth, nor anything else in all creation, will be able to separate us from the love of God that is in Christ Jesus our Lord." This illness cannot separate you from the love of God; nor the vile thought placed in your head by hell or the powers that are at war against you. Satan is a fallen angel and he cannot separate you from the love of God that is in Christ Jesus. That is truth; it is rock solid.

Philippians 1:6, "Being confident of this, that he who began a good work in you will carry it on to completion until the day of Christ Jesus." When God saved you, He began a good work in you, and is in the process of completing it. This may be the furnace that He is using to refine you, but you are kept by His hands.

CHAPTER SIX

SUICIDE

The prevalence of mental illness and suicide has been dramatically underreported, convincing many to believe those who are mentally ill are few and far between, and that the occurrence of suicide is infrequent. According to the CDC, "There were 38,364 suicides in 2010 in the United States—an average of 105 each day. Suicide was the tenth leading cause of death for all ages in 2010. Suicide results in an estimated $34.6 billion in combined medical and work loss costs."[24]

The National Alliance on Mental Health reports, "Over 90 percent of people who commit suicide have been diagnosed with mental illness."[25] In a report issued by the US Surgeon General and the National Action Alliance for Suicide Prevention, it was stated, "Suicidal behavior among mood disorder patients occur almost exclusively during an acute, severe, major depressive episode." [26] The evidence that links mental illness and suicide is staggering. The physical evidence proves that the suffering of those with mental illness goes way beyond the normal, everyday ups and downs.

Satan is a deceiver, liar, and murderer. In 2 Corinthians 11:14, the Bible says, "For Satan himself masquerades as an angel of light." He tempts us to doubt God. He uses our thoughts, our senses, and our circumstances against us. He lies and tells us there is no danger in following him. From Genesis to Revelation, we see Satan employing these tactics.

In Genesis, Satan tempted Eve to doubt by saying, "Did God really say …?" (Genesis 3:1). He used her sight, appetite, and proximity to the tree to tempt her to eat the fruit. He gently coerced her into thinking there was no danger by saying, "You will not surely die" (Genesis 3:4). He lied and told her that it would benefit her to eat the fruit.

Satan devastated Job's life and then tempted him to doubt God's love for him. Job says of God, "My opponent fastens on me his piercing eyes" (Job 16:9). His feelings deceived him, making him believe God was his enemy.

Satan tempted Jesus in the wilderness after He had fasted for forty days and nights. He used Jesus' hunger against Him. He told Jesus that there would be no harm if He jumped off the temple because the angels would catch Him. Satan used the sense of sight to tempt Jesus with all the kingdoms of the world (Matthew 4:1–11).

In Revelation, Satan is described as using visual signs and miracles to deceive the whole world. He lies, persuading the world into thinking that there is safety in accepting the mark and worshipping the Beast.

Today, Satan plots and schemes against the physically depressed and mentally ill. He causes us to doubt our salvation, God's love, and God's faithfulness. He shoots his fiery darts into our minds. He disguises his thoughts as our thoughts and uses them and our feelings against us. He strikes when we are critically ill, are tired, can't sleep, can't think, and are in isolation. He takes advantage of our illness, using visual and auditory hallucinations to tempt us, causing fear and alarm. He lies to us and tells us that everyone will be better off if we end our lives, that there are no consequences, and that suicide is safe. He comes as an angel of light, encouraging us to end our suffering.

Satan deceives the church into believing there is no such thing as physical depression. He lies and tells us all depression stems from issues of the heart. We are fooled into thinking there is no problem in our church. Everyone looks and sounds healthy. Certainly we would be able to tell if someone had depression. He lulls us into thinking that there is no danger in the church, that Christians are immune from mental illness. And when deceiving, lying, murderous Satan does succeed in tempting an ill brother or sister into taking his or her own life, he uses that event to cause even more devastation.

My mind tormented me. My illness erased who I was. I was a mere shadow of myself. I was distantly familiar with the outside world, but eye contact with others became uncomfortable. I thought they could see in my eyes that I was not the same person anymore.

I felt that I had been hijacked in my own body. Like I had been taken away to some distant place within myself, and the disturbing thoughts and ominous feelings had taken over. No matter how hard I tried to push those thoughts and feelings out, it was impossible. My situation was unbearable.

My husband kept a gun upstairs for home security. I had fleeting thoughts about the gun, and that scared me. I didn't want those thoughts, and I certainly didn't welcome them or entertain them, but they came. The thoughts of using the gun seemed as inconsequential as popping a bag of popcorn. To my ill brain they didn't register as a significant act. That also scared me.

My headaches only got worse as I tried to figure it all out. I thought, *Just one shot and my headache would be gone.* In a detached consciousness, I knew then that I was in real danger. When I was in college I took a psychiatric nursing class that taught me if someone tells you he or she has a plan for suicide, you should take that statement seriously. I applied that to myself. I knew I was in trouble.

One afternoon, I was alone in my bed when I had a gentle urging to get up, go to my husband's dresser, and get his gun. I felt like I actually watched myself doing that, almost as if I hallucinated doing it. It appeared to be a safe thought to me at the time, as if I would go from fighting to silence, from pain to peace.

How awful, I thought. I wanted someone to see what I was enduring, but that was impossible. I was scared and knew I was in danger, but I was too embarrassed to let anyone know what was really going on. It was horrible and unbelievable.

Finally, I thought, *I have to put down my pride and just tell him*. I called my husband upstairs. "You need to hide your gun," I told him with my eyes closed, too embarrassed to look at him.

"You're kidding," he replied.

"No, I'm not," I answered. He proceeded to hide his gun from me. I didn't tell him anything else. The episode passed.

Another time I was standing in the kitchen, looking out the window. It was a relatively normal day. Unexpectedly, I thought I heard a gentle voice telling me that God wanted me home now. I had a prompting, a hallucinatory false call, that He wanted me in a safe place. The urging was almost physical, like someone was helping me in that direction. This time, God gave me a strong conviction based on His truth, that he didn't need me to help Him accomplish anything. He didn't need me to send myself to Him; if he wanted me home, He would bring me there. By the power of God I was able to resist the urge. This also passed.

In Albert Hsu's book *Grieving a Suicide*, he shares his personal grief over the death of his father, Terri. His father was an immigrant from Taiwan, an independent, self-made man who, through his expertise in computer technology, received top-level security clearance to work on government contracts. He was a well-respected innovator. He suffered a stroke which led to depression. He began to have feelings of guilt, hopelessness, loss of perspective, and failure. His mind became so distorted by the illness of severe clinical depression that he ended his life by suicide.

Mr. Hsu says, "Ironically, suicide is a kind of survival mechanism. Most suicides are undertaken as a way to escape the unbearable pain of depression. The depression has so distorted the victim's perception that they are hardly aware that the act of suicide will cause untold grief for their loved ones; the focus is simply on escaping the pain and despair. The agony of depression is so great that the suicide musters the resolve to do away with the pain, at the expense of his or her own life." [27]

Early in the book of Matthew, we read about the temptations of Jesus. I want to focus on the way in which the Devil offered up his second temptation. Jesus had been fasting for forty days and nights when the Devil came to tempt Him. "Then the devil took him to the holy city and had him stand on the highest point of the temple. 'If you are the Son of God,' he said, 'throw yourself down. For it is written: "He will command his angels concerning you, and they will lift you up in their hands, so that you will not strike your foot against a stone"'" (Matthew 4:5–7).

The devil was quoting from Psalms, where the psalmist is talking about the security and protection the believer has when he trusts and obeys God. Psalm 91:11 says, "For He will command his angels concerning you to guard you in all your ways; they will lift you up in their hands, so that you will not strike your foot against a stone." When we fully trust and obey God, He will protect us in all our ways. There is safety in obeying God.

Satan was urging Jesus to perform an impressive, angelic spectacle. The reality was he wanted to destroy God's plan, but the temptation was wrapped in the illusion of safety and protection. There would be no harm because angels would catch Jesus. There would be no consequence; His foot wouldn't even touch the ground. The Devil used trickery when he presented the temptation by making it appear that there was no danger in the action.

About this passage, Matthew Henry says, "The devil would persuade Christ to throw himself down, hoping that He would be His own murderer, and that there would be an end of Him and His undertaking, which he looked upon with a jealous eye; to encourage Him to do it, he tells Him, that there was no danger, that the good angels would protect Him, for so was the promise." [28]

The Devil's proposal to Jesus was not unlike the proposition he made to Eve in the garden. Eve's acquiescence to her temptation brought death. Jesus, however, flatly refused Satan's proposal, using God's Word to overcome the Evil One. "Jesus answered him, 'It is also written: "Do not put the Lord your God to the test" (Matthew 4:7). Jesus' response to those temptations displayed the power of God's Word to defeat the darkest powers of evil.

This is why the study of the Devil's method of the temptation of Jesus is important to the subject of suicide. The Devil wraps his poison in pretty packages. He cannot make you sin, but he can make sin look good. He can entice you toward an action that gives a false impression of goodness and safety. We need to be aware of his schemes because the Devil wants to destroy us and God's plan for us.

Satan works against the mentally ill in the same way. Buried within the hallucinations and promptings is the Devil's desire to destroy God's plan for our lives. When I was severely depressed and in crisis, the temptation was not to commit suicide; it was to obey the false but seemingly real call of God to go home. The temptation to act is not processed by the illness as being selfish or having consequences. In the moment, it seemed that an external source was luring me to a safe place, blocking all appropriate ancillary thoughts. The enemy came, disguised as an angel of light, tempting me to act by lying that God wanted me home.

Jesus' example in rejecting the Devil's proposition is a model for us. Hebrews 4:12 says, "For the Word of God is living and active. Sharper than any double-edged sword, it penetrates even to dividing soul and spirit, joints and marrow." God's Word is our weapon against the temptation of suicide. Bible memory is crucial, because the Devil doesn't give you warning when he will attack. God's Word, the sword of the Spirit, needs to be firmly planted in your mind so that when the temptation comes, you will be prepared to use it.

But more than that, this is the benefit we as believers have. We have the living Lord Jesus who stands guard over our lives and always provides a way of escape. "No temptation has seized you except what is common to man. And God is faithful; he will not let you be tempted beyond what you can bear. But when you are tempted, he will also provide a way out so that you can stand up under it" (1 Corinthians 10:13).

Some brothers and sisters have had severe depression for much longer than I have. In my case, I found a combination of medicines that helped my depression to lift. Some do not, and they live with this agony for years. There have been people serving in ministry who, after suffering with this illness, have ended their lives in the tragedy of suicide. Their tragedies, however, were lived out in their ill minds. The act of suicide just gives evidence to the cruelty of what they suffered.

I have experienced this illness, but I do not know the grief of suicide. Albert Hsu states, "Without excusing their act, we can say what Jesus said on the cross: 'Father forgive them, for they know not what they do.' Those who choose suicide usually don't realize how much trauma and grief they inflict on us survivors. Even though we feel hurt, angry and betrayed, we can come to forgive them because their final thoughts were preoccupied with ending their own pain. They did not know what they were doing to us." [29]

CHAPTER SEVEN

THE STORM AND THE ROCK

Do you remember the old Sunday School song, "The wise man built his house upon a rock"? When the storm came, the wise man's house stood firm and the foolish man's house crumbled.

Well, the storm of depression affects the whole house, not just the ill family member. The ill family member certainly suffers a great deal, but when one person has severe depression, the whole family is affected. The illness permeates the attitudes of everyone in the home. The source is singular, but depression's menacing thoughts and attitudes infiltrate the home. It is the "perfect storm" for the Enemy to use to attack the family.

"Divide and conquer" is a military strategy used to break up a larger group into smaller ones. The same strategy makes it easier for the Enemy to take us down piece by piece. First, he divides the sufferers of depression from the local body of believers. He does this using our pride. We don't want anyone to know we are suffering, so we keep it a secret and forego the prayer support and love. Second, he divides us in our homes. The physically depressed person's mind can't process information, and well family members have difficulty understanding what their loved one is going through. They hurl their frustrations at each other as the stress mounts.

A family struggling with this illness can be encouraged if they can step back and realize that their ill family member is not the enemy. "For our struggle is not against flesh and blood, but against rulers, against the authorities, against the powers of this dark world and against the spiritual forces of evil in the heavenly realms" (Ephesians 6:12). The family is in a battle with an unseen Enemy who is bent on destroying their family. Realizing there are outside forces working against them, the family can then recognize and identify the real Enemy.

Confusion is another tactic used by the military to frustrate and demoralize an opponent. Depression does this too. We cannot gauge how sick an individual is by any lab work, test, or scan. The only way we can determine how ill someone is, is by actions and attitudes. This is hard on every home in which a depressed person lives. "Is he acting this way out of rebellion, or is it his illness?" A husband might think, "Is she really sick, or does she just not want to cook?" A wife might think, "We used to go out all the time, and now he won't do anything but sit around the house and watch TV all day! I don't know if it's his illness or if he's just being lazy." In 1 Corinthians 14:33, the Bible says, "For God is not the author of confusion, but of peace" (KJV).

Depression demands much from the family—patience, self-sacrifice, time. We may have the expectation of a quick recovery once a diagnosis is made, because the depressed family member is now taking medication. Other than his behavior, everything else about the depressed person looks perfectly fine. But inside the ill family member's brain, things are not fine. The family may have to adjust its schedule and be flexible to meet the needs of the ill member. The family will need space to absorb the impact of the illness. They might need to share what's going on with trusted relatives and friends, asking for prayer and help. They may even need to take temporary leave from external responsibilities to tend to their ill family member. The stress of this illness on a family can be oppressive. Alleviating unnecessary stress helps to ease the burden.

The family can easily be drained of love and patience as it works to fill the void that the depressed family member leaves when he or she becomes ill. As family members help out and empty themselves of their own strength to help the depressed loved one, they feel the need to escape and recharge their own batteries. This strain on a family can be alleviated by the body of Christ. The family can be lifted by comfort, prayer, and an understanding ear.

When families come to church after a long week of battling through this illness, they may want to scream, "Is everybody's life going fine? Mine sure isn't!" Small talk, meaningless fluff, and the quick and passing "Hey, how are ya's" just remind them that they are really alone in the midst of a lot of well-meaning saints. We need to fill all people up with love, not knowing who is suffering, being sensitive not to criticize.

Obedience is a choice, but it is not always the easiest path. Love one another. In John 13:34–35, Jesus says, "A new command I give you: Love one another. As I have loved you, so you must love one another. By this all men will know that you are my disciples, if you love one another." God is so good to tell His children to love one another, not to judge. We should carry each other's burdens. If we, the church, would remind ourselves to act this way out of obedience and love for God, we would heal families coping with depression and not hurt them.

I remember feeling that I was somehow out of God's provision and protection. Mental illness was an area that the church had not accepted. I believed mental illness was the only slice of the human experience that was not addressed by the church. In fact, it was probably avoided out of an unconscious sense of self-preservation.

When we do not understand things, we typically want to avoid them. It feels more comfortable to stay with the familiar; it is a natural instinct. We feel fearful when we consider the realm of the mentally ill in the context of God's Word. It is not cut and dried, so we would rather pretend it doesn't exist.

Mental illness is totally exposed before God. Its manifestations are clearly understood by Him. "Nothing in all creation is hidden from God's sight. Everything is uncovered and laid bare before the eyes of Him to whom we must give account" (Hebrews 4:13). The temptation is to give in to desperation during the storm, when we look out the window and there is only darkness, when we find no place to share the burden of this illness in an atmosphere of acceptance and love. But we do have a place to bring our burdens and find acceptance and love: the Rock of our salvation. During the storm, He is the only one who can keep our house from falling. Jesus is our Rock. He is the living Word of God. When I was clinging to those words of comfort from my mom, my mother-in-law, and my husband, I was clinging to the Rock in them. Let Jesus allow you to be a Rock for others in their storms. Be there as a support.

God used this storm in my life to refine me. It was very painful. "In this you greatly rejoice, though now for a little while you may have had to suffer grief in all kinds of trials. These have come so that your faith—of greater worth than gold, which perishes even though refined by fire—may be proved genuine and may result in praise, glory and honor when Jesus Christ is revealed" (1 Peter 1:6–7). While we are unaware of the reasons or purposes for our sufferings, God is in control of the temperature gauge. He knows how hot it needs to be. He refines us to make us vessels through which He can display His glory. We can trust Him in our storms, and we can believe Him as we go through the fire. He is faithful and He is good.

Hebrews 4:15 says, "For we do not have a high priest who is unable to sympathize with our weaknesses, but we have one who has been tempted in every way, just as we are—yet was without sin." Jesus has compassion like no one else. He knows how we feel. Isaiah 53:3–5 describes for us the suffering that Jesus endured:

> He was despised and rejected by men, a man of sorrows, and familiar with suffering. Like one from whom men hide their faces he was despised, and we esteemed him not. Surely he took up our infirmities and carried our sorrows, yet we considered Him stricken by God, smitten by Him, and afflicted. But He was pierced for our transgressions, He was crushed for our iniquities; the punishment that brought us peace was upon Him, and by His wounds we are healed.

Jesus was a man of sorrows, and knows what it is to suffer. It was for God's eternal purpose that Jesus suffered. Suffering does not mean abandonment. Please do not abandon a family because of the stigma associated with depression.

Deuteronomy 31:6 says, "Be strong and courageous. Do not be afraid or terrified because of them, for the LORD your God goes with you; He will never leave you nor forsake you." Even in the pit, He goes there with you. We should not be afraid to go with others into their pit; it is a comfort to them when people are willing to share in their grief.

Deuteronomy 31:8 says, "The Lord himself goes before you and will be with you; he will never leave you nor forsake you. Do not be afraid; do not be discouraged." The Lord Himself goes before us. We cannot go beyond His care. We might not know how God leads His children who have physical depression, but He leads them. He is the good Shepherd; He never abandons one of His sheep.

Psalm 139:5 says, "You hem me in—behind and before; you have laid your hand upon me." Not only does the Lord go before us, He also is behind us. We are not alone.

Deuteronomy 33:27 says, "The eternal God is your refuge, and underneath are the everlasting arms." God is before us and behind us. Even though we feel like we are in the deepest pit, His arms are underneath us.

Isaiah 41:10 says, "So do not fear, for I am with you; do not be dismayed, for I am your God. I will strengthen you and help you; I will uphold you with my righteous right hand." When we collapse and it's all we can do to breathe, we call out to God. His righteous right hand does not grow weary. He will give us the strength we need.

> I have loved you with an everlasting love; I have drawn you with loving-kindness. I will build you up again and you will be rebuilt, O Virgin Israel. Again you will take up your tambourines and go out to dance with the joyful. Again you

will plant vineyards on the hills of Samaria; the
farmers will plant them and enjoy their fruit.
There will be a day when watchmen cry out
on the hills of Ephraim, "Come, let us go up to
Zion, to the LORD our God." (Jeremiah 31:3–6)

There is a future hope. As hopeless as depression feels,
it is true that one day those who are in Christ will take up
tambourines and dance. We will leave these mortal bodies and
be given new ones. This illness will one day be done away with.

Below are some verses for reflection as we remember
how God cares for His children. As we are reminded of
His goodness and gentleness, we can reflect His love and
encouragement to our brothers and sisters struggling with
depression.

The LORD is close to the brokenhearted and
saves those who are crushed in spirit. (Psalm
34:18)

God is our refuge and strength, an ever-present
help in trouble. (Psalm 46:1)

In the same way, the Spirit helps us in our
weakness. We do not know what we ought to
pray for, but the Spirit himself intercedes for
us with groans that words cannot express.
(Romans 8:26)

The LORD lifts up those who are bowed down. (Psalm 146:8)

When you pass through the waters, I will be with you; and when you pass through the rivers, they will not sweep over you. When you walk through the fire, you will not be burned; the flames will not set you ablaze. (Isaiah 43:2)

In this world you will have trouble. But take heart! I have overcome the world. (John 16:33)

As you know, we consider blessed those who have persevered. You have heard of Job's perseverance and have seen what the Lord finally brought about. The Lord is full of compassion and mercy. (James 5:11)

The rain came down, the streams rose, and the winds blew and beat against that house; yet it did not fall, because it had its foundation on the rock. (Matthew 7:25)

The Solid Rock
by Edward Mote, 1834

My hope is built on nothing less
Than Jesus' blood and righteousness;
I dare not trust the sweetest frame,
But wholly lean on Jesus' name.

On Christ, the solid rock, I stand-
All other ground is sinking sand,
All other ground is sinking sand.

When darkness veils His lovely face,
I rest on His unchanging grace;
In ev'ry high and stormy gale,
My anchor holds within the veil.

His oath, His covenant, His blood,
Support me in the whelming flood;
When all around my soul gives way,
He then is all my hope and stay.

CHAPTER EIGHT

YIELDING

I felt like I had experienced an undiscovered illness, a terrible and cruel illness that attacked my faith, my family, and my whole being. I was embarrassed that I had suffered such an unpopular and misunderstood illness. I felt shame and wanted to protect myself from being labeled as someone with a mental illness. I wanted to put this whole experience behind me and move on.

At first my goal was to wean myself off the medication. I tried many times, and I was unsuccessful each time. The same symptoms would come back, and I would feel defeated. More recently, I have accepted that this illness is a part of my life. The Lord has not healed me but has graciously provided me with the tools I need to manage my depression well. Romans 8:28

says, "And we know that in all things God works for the good of those who love him, who have been called according to His purpose." God's Word says that He works in all things, which includes all bad things. In this bad illness, God was working for His good purposes.

I am the steward of the body that God gave me. I need to manage my depression well so that I can produce fruit for God's kingdom. The jobs that God has given me haven't changed, but my health has. I am still a wife and mother and want to be a good example to my children. I can't do that without taking medication.

In Matthew 25:14–30, Jesus tells the parable of the talents. A man was an owner of land. Before going on a journey, he called his three servants and gave them the responsibility for his property and his talents, or coins. Jesus says, "The man who had received the five talents went at once and put his money to work and gained five more. So also, the one with two talents gained two more. But the man who had received the one talent went off, dug a hole in the ground and hid his master's money" (vv. 16–18).

When the owner returned, there was an accounting of what the servants had done with their talents. The first two servants multiplied theirs, were rewarded with more, and were invited to share in their master's happiness. The third servant buried his talent in the ground and paid no heed to it. The owner was angry at this servant. Jesus says, "Take the talent from him and give it to the one who has the ten talents. For everyone who has will be given more and he will have an abundance. Whoever does not have, even what he has will be taken from him. And throw that worthless servant outside, into the darkness, where there will be weeping and gnashing of teeth" (vv. 28–30).

In this parable, Jesus is teaching that He is the owner of this world, and He gave us our lives to live. He also gave us His Word, the Bible, which tells us that He will come back one day and will require an accounting of what He gave us. What did we spend our years investing in? Did we invest our time on constructing our images, chasing financial security, accumulating material possessions, and ensuring our own pleasure? Or did we spend our years in humble submission to Jesus, serving and building up the kingdom of God?

In the light of eternity, our pride and our plans are meaningless. Having a singular allegiance to Jesus Christ is all that matters. Those of us who love the Lord Jesus Christ and have suffered can lay aside our pride and lift up others who are struggling with depression. Our experience and insight can be a comfort. God uses these trials to transform us into His image so that we can be used by Him to encourage and strengthen others for His glory.

In 1 Thessalonians 5:14, Paul urges the church to "encourage the timid, help the weak, be patient with everyone." If you see signs that a family is suffering with depression, be an encourager. Ephesians 2:10 says, "For we are God's workmanship, created in Christ Jesus to do good works, which God prepared in advance for us to do." If you have suffered through physical depression, you know how hard it is on a family. Be willing to share your story with others who are struggling through their depression.

We are here on earth for a short while. The owner is coming back and will want an accounting of our talents. Let us be ready and have an abundance to show Him.

Have Thine Own Way, Lord
by Adelaide A. Pollard 1907

Have Thine own way, Lord! Have Thine own way!
Thou art the Potter, I am the clay.
Mold me and make me after Thy will,
While I am waiting, yielded and still.

Have Thine own way, Lord! Have Thine own way!
Search me and try me, Master today!
Whiter than snow, Lord, wash me just now,
As in Thy presence humbly I bow.

Have Thine own way, Lord! Have Thine own way!
Wounded and weary, help me, I pray!
Power all power surely is Thine!
Touch me and heal me, Savior divine!

Have Thine own way, Lord! Have Thine own way!
Hold o'er my being absolute sway!
Fill with Thy Spirit till all shall see
Christ only, always, living in me!

CHAPTER NINE

TO THE CHURCH

I have lived with physical depression for about ten years. Before I developed depression, I was uninformed and had an opinion about depression based on my understanding of sin, God's discipline of sin, and the effects of guilt. My opinion was also based on my experience of being a healthy individual, one who personally did not know anyone with the illness of physical depression. Never considering any explanation other than the spiritual, I assumed that people who went to doctors to solve their problems were not spiritual. I believed that if they spent more time in God's Word, they might not need the doctors.

This perspective was radically challenged after my third son was born. Something was terribly wrong, alarmingly wrong. I was given a diagnosis that I immediately rejected. I was given medication that I refused. My health started to decline after I had used all my spiritual resources. I became aware that I was in deep trouble and had to do something.

I started taking the medication even while being skeptical that it would help. As my health slowly improved, I also began to understand that my previous opinion that all depression was spiritual was wrong. It was formed in ignorance.

According to LifeWay Research, "A third of Americans— and nearly half of evangelical, fundamentalist, or born-again Christians—believe prayer and Bible study alone can overcome serious mental illness." [30] This was my previous opinion of depression, and it caused untold troubles to my health and my recovery. This opinion continues to flourish in the church today.

In the book of Job, God allows Satan to attack Job. Job is described as "blameless and upright; He feared God and shunned evil" (Job 1:1). Satan wanted to prove that the only reason Job lived a life that pleased God was because God had blessed and protected him.

Job's life became a battle point, unbeknownst to him. He lost his children, his possessions, and his health. Job 2:7 says, "Satan went out from the presence of the Lord and afflicted Job with painful sores from the soles of his feet to the top of his head." Job's friends, upon seeing him, were speechless for seven days. His friends saw his great loss, looked upon his terrible sores, and drew a conclusion: God was punishing him for some sin. They condemned him because of how Job's circumstances appeared.

Job 42:7-8 says,

> After the LORD had said these things to Job, he
> said to Eliphaz the Temanite, "I am angry with
> you and your two friends, because you have
> not spoken of Me what is right, as my servant
> Job has. So now take seven bulls and seven
> rams and go to my servant Job and sacrifice a
> burnt offering for yourselves. My servant Job
> will pray for you, and I will accept his prayer
> and not deal with you according to your folly.
> You have not spoken of Me what is right as my
> servant Job has."

According to *Matthew Henry's Commentary*, Job's three friends "had censured and condemned Job upon a false hypothesis, had represented God fighting against Job as an enemy when really He was only trying him as a friend, and this was not right." [31]

Henry also goes on to explain, "It is a dangerous thing to judge uncharitably of the spiritual and eternal state of others, for in so doing we may perhaps condemn those whom God has accepted, which is a great provocation to Him; it is offending His little ones, and He takes Himself to be wronged in all the wrongs that are done to them." [32] They judged Job based on appearances.

In John 7:24, Jesus said to the Jews, "Stop judging by mere appearances, and make a right judgment." The Jews allowed the work of circumcision to be performed on the Sabbath but were angry with Jesus for the work of healing a man on the Sabbath. The Jews were judging wrongly because their hearts were far from God. We can please God by asking the Holy Spirit to examine our motivations and our fears.

Antidepressant medication can be a stumbling block for many believers because they feel that the choice is between God and medicine. That is assuming too much. That is assuming there is no such thing as physical depression. The choice a believer must make when he has this illness is whether to believe that God wants to condemn him for his illness or to believe that He is a God of mercy. The Devil would have us believe that God wants to condemn us.

Sometimes we don't know what to think about an issue with which we are not familiar. James 2:13 says, "Mercy triumphs over judgment!" Mercy is not equal to judgment. It is victorious over judgment. It should be part of who we are as Christians: being full of mercy. "Be merciful, just as your Father is merciful" (Luke 6:36).

God used this illness to change me. This was an illness I previously saw through a fog of misconception and misunderstanding. Through life experiences, we learn and we grow. Once-solid ideas or opinions can change over time. We will never cease to learn on this side of heaven.

I want to stimulate thinking within the church, to evaluate entrenched prejudices. We may, with introspection, determine that these opinions developed innocently, out of ignorance. We may realize that we were judging things we didn't really understand. Allow the Holy Spirit to lead you in this area.

The church is divided on this topic. There are those who believe all depression is spiritual, and there are those who believe that, while there is spiritual discouragement, also referred to as depression, there is likewise a physical illness called depression that can be successfully treated with medicine and other therapies. Paul, in his letter to the church at Corinth, said, "I appeal to you, brothers, in the name of our Lord Jesus Christ, that all of you agree with one another so that there may be no divisions among you and that you may be perfectly united in mind and thought" (1 Corinthians 1:10). This illness is used by the Devil as a divisive tool that may cause discord among believers. It may cause hurt, confusion, and isolation. But we have the Holy Spirit, and we can ask Him to guide us in all things. I pray that the Holy Spirit will soften hearts and open eyes.

We cannot let Satan outwit us by using this illness against us. Be aware of his schemes and stand on truth in the face of all that mentally ill people may do or say. Do not be intimidated. Though their thoughts and feelings are strong and sincere, their illness has impaired their best attempts at rational thought. God's Word is truth, and you can help severely depressed people by gently reaffirming the truth. Remembering that their brains are not functioning normally; do not allow their delusions or affected thinking to cause you to become confused or to doubt the truth.

This illness may be problematic for some church counselors. When Bible study and prayer alone cannot alleviate the symptoms, it can be confusing and intimidating. If you are counseling someone who is cooperating but unable to find relief, you may be dealing with something more than just a spiritual issue. While a depressed person may need to seek medical assistance, it does not mean that he or she should give up spiritual counsel. It may be that the brain and body need to be adjusted so that the spirit can be relieved of the heavy burden of this illness.

The symptoms of physical depression stem from a brain that is out of balance and not functioning normally. Unalleviated guilt, constant confession, evil thoughts, feelings of judgment, doubt, loss of peace, loss of hope: these are normal feelings that we all struggle with from time to time. Physical depression causes these normal feelings to be simultaneous, intense, unrelenting, and significantly out of proportion as compared to how they are experienced by the healthy individual. While our ability to think and concentrate is interrupted, and while our bodies experience extreme exhaustion, our minds are constantly harassed by these overwhelming feelings.

These symptoms exasperate the Christian who is trying to fight back with prayer and Bible study. The symptoms confuse those close to physically depressed people because, in the context of their lives, their expressed thoughts and behaviors are highly unusual. This is because the source is physical. When we ask God to search our hearts, He is always faithful to reveal our specific transgressions to us. When a person's behavior changes, he experiences these symptoms in an inconsolable way, and he is unable to discern the source, then it may be wise to suggest that he see a doctor.

God's Word speaks of medicine as a means of healing and recovery. Proverbs 31:6–7 says, "Give strong drink unto him that is ready to perish, and wine unto those that be of heavy hearts. Let him drink, and forget his poverty, and remember his misery no more" (KJV). It is clear that there is a provision in God's Word for the medicinal use of wine as refreshment and relief to the one who is suffering in the physical body and to the one suffering with mental anguish or distress.

When we make general statements that Christians should not take antidepressants, we are positioning ourselves against those brothers and sisters who are taking medication to treat their depression. When we take a stand against those brothers and sisters who take antidepressants, those whom God desires to comfort, we misrepresent Jesus to the church and to the world. "Praise be to the God and Father of our Lord Jesus Christ, the Father of compassion and the God of all comfort, who comforts us in all our troubles, so that we can comfort those in any trouble with the comfort we ourselves have received from God" (2 Corinthians 1:3–4).

As believers, we are all the recipients of God's great mercy. We owed a great debt that we could not pay. Through faith in the death, burial, and resurrection of Jesus, God paid our debt. In Matthew 18:21–35, we read of a man who could not pay a debt and begged for mercy. This man was given mercy and his debt was canceled. He then went out to collect a small debt from his servant. The servant begged for mercy, and the man refused. The master was very angry because he had given mercy and canceled the man's great debt, and this man refused to give his own servant mercy over a small debt. "In anger his master turned him over to the jailers to be tortured until he should pay back all he owed" (Matthew 18:34).

We have been given mercy that we do not deserve. Let us honor God and extend that mercy to others, as He would have us do. The mercy that we have received, we can show to others. "Praise be to the God and Father of our Lord Jesus Christ! In his great mercy He has given us new birth into a living hope through the resurrection of Jesus Christ from the dead, and into an inheritance that can never perish, spoil or fade—kept in heaven for you, who through faith are shielded by God's power until the coming of the salvation that is ready to be revealed in the last time" (1 Peter 1:3–5). Let us not forget the great mercy that has been given to us as we deal with one another. Instead, "Be imitators of God, therefore, as dearly loved children and live a life of love, just as Christ loved us and gave himself up for us as a fragrant offering and sacrifice to God" (Ephesians 5:1–2).

God is honored when we treat our suffering brothers and sisters with respect. Titus 3:12 says, "Remind the people to be subject to rulers and authorities, to be obedient, to be ready to do whatever is good, to slander no one, to be peaceable and considerate, and to show true humility toward all men." Those who struggle with depression, along with their families, have invisible wounds and have suffered much. It honors God to treat them and their families with humility and respect. Remember that God allows trials to refine our faith. Treat these families going through this trial with acceptance, gentleness, and love.

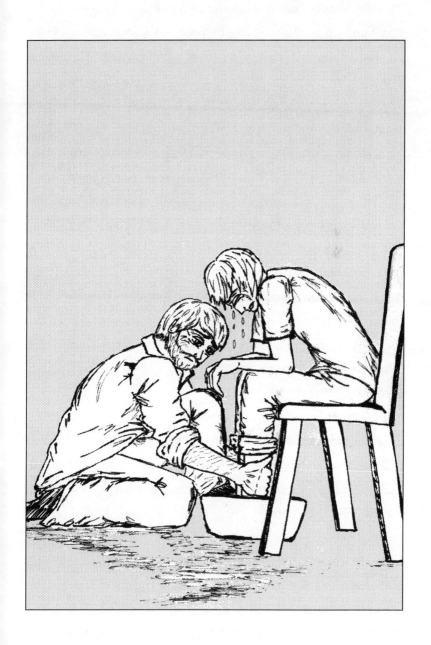

Galatians 6:2 says, "Carry each other's burdens, and in this way you will fulfill the law of Christ." We don't have to know all the details of someone's illness to help carry his burden. There are many practical ways to help people struggling with depression. They may be tired; their bodies do not have the strength they used to have. You can help out with simple things: carpooling, meals, an offer to babysit or cut the grass. You could offer help in fulfilling obligations they may have.

You can also help by listening. Give someone the space to grieve. Listening allows him to talk, and talking allows him to sort things out. This is important for the family members of the depressed person, too. They are exhausted, and family life has been turned upside down. They, too, could use someone to carry their burdens. Alleviating their responsibilities frees them up to care for their suffering loved one. Comforting them fills them up, so they can continue to pour into their loved one.

When the body of Christ comes around these families, covering them and their loved ones with prayer, love, acceptance, and support, it shows the world who Jesus is. It strengthens the family that is under attack. It encourages those who serve the family because there is great joy in serving. It makes God happy to see His children loving one another and obeying His Word by carrying each other's burdens. When we support the feeble arms of those who are depressed and their families, we are in fact holding up Jesus. "The King will reply, 'I tell you the truth, whatever you did for one of the least of these brothers of mine, you did for Me'" (Matthew 25:40).

I beg the church of Jesus Christ to see the pain in your congregations. It is there. We have driven it underground for long enough by our attitudes of unfair judgment. Change your hearts. Start believing those brothers and sisters who say they suffer from physical depression or any other mental illness. Do not dismiss their valid claims because those claims don't fit in with your theology. "Do not judge, or you too will be judged. For in the same way you judge others, you will be judged, and with the measure you use, it will be measured to you" (Matthew 7:1–2).

Let us determine to put off judgment and put on mercy toward our brothers and sisters who suffer from physical depression. Let us be kind and compassionate. Let us determine to honor God in our attitudes and conduct toward these families in order to strengthen and build up the kingdom of God. We are the servants of the living God; let us serve the wounded among us. In humility, let us turn from old prejudices to accept and love those struggling with this illness. "Accept one another then, just as Christ accepted you, in order to bring praise to God" (Romans 15:7).

We Can Change
by Alison Hall 2013

I did not see you standing there,
with your down cast eyes and your feelings bare.
I did not look when you passed my way,
'cause I did not know; 'cause you did not say.

I want to know, I want to hear,
I realized not, enlightened, I care.
I will not ignore what I misunderstood.
I won't avoid, or fear to learn; I could.

I will confront the thing I did not know.
I will inspect again, this thing, your foe.
I will not judge this burden that you bear.
Lean on my arm, my strength I'll gladly share.

I too have much that you don't know,
I too have burdens that don't show.
But we have His strength and access to His throne,
We can comfort one another that this world is not our home.

DISCUSSION QUESTIONS

Chapters One and Two:
Were you surprised that depression could be the source of all the symptoms that were mentioned in chapters one and two?

How would you have dealt with this illness?

Would you have recognized the symptoms earlier than I did?

Chapter Three:
Can you see how easily our adversary could confuse a Christian struggling with this illness?

Is there any person in your church who speaks openly or plainly about an experience with depression?

What teachings or opinions about depression are vocalized in your church?

Does the message you hear make people with this illness feel safe to share their difficulties?

Chapter Four:
Do you find it difficult to believe a Christian can be so ill that it can disrupt his trust and faith in God?

Does the lack of our ability diminish the truth of God's Word?

Chapter Five:
Is all guilt a result of sin?

Can a Christian experience false guilt? Where does false guilt come from?

What would you advise a person to do when he had confessed to sin but continues to feel crushed by guilt?

What does Jesus say He will do when we confess our sins?

What is the unpardonable sin?

Chapter Six
If someone mentioned to you that he was having suicidal thoughts, what would you do?

Can a Christian be deceived into thinking a sinful act will be safe and good?

When you hear of someone committing suicide, what is your normal response?

Can the surviving family members tell you what was going on in the mind of their loved one?

How would you feel if you had to explain a family member's illness in the middle of your grief?

Chapter Seven:
When is the best time to build your house on the Rock, before or during a storm?

Name two ways the adversary can use this illness to break apart a home.

How can the church build up a family who is battle weary?

How would you respond if you knew a family was struggling with a severely depressed member?

Chapter Eight:
What is your view on antidepressants and other medical treatments for depression?

Do you feel that an antidepressant would interfere with a person's spiritual life? Why or why not?

Do you think it is wrong to alleviate mental suffering with medication?

Do you think it is wrong to alleviate physical suffering with medication?

Chapter Nine:
What has been your opinion of depression?

Do you think God loves the healthy and happy in heart more than the depressed and crushed in spirit?

Which type of person is more valuable to Him?

Could your spoken opinion of depression have hurt or hindered the treatment of someone with severe depression?

What triumphs over judgment? (James 2:13)

When you serve the least of these, who are you really serving? (Matthew 25:40)

What would it cost you to be merciful and lovingly accept someone suffering with physical depression?

What did it cost Jesus to be merciful and lovingly accept those who come to Him through faith?

Note from the Author

Dear Reader,

If you have been reading this book and do not know Jesus Christ as your Lord and Savior, then this note is for you. The feelings of hopelessness that come with the illness of depression are overwhelming and devastating. Beyond the feelings, however, is truth. God's Word is truth. God's Word teaches that true and lasting hope is only found in Jesus Christ. He alone can offer you the forgiveness of sins, a new beginning, and eternal life. I was once presented with these truths found in the Bible.

"For all have sinned and fall short of the glory of God" (Romans 3:23). The Bible also states, "As it is written: 'There is no one righteous, not even one'" (Romans 3:10). I believed that I was a sinner and that my sin separated me from God.

"For the wages of sin is death, but the gift of God is eternal life in Christ Jesus our Lord" (Romans 6:2, 3). I understood that the punishment for my sin was death, eternal separation from God. I understood that God offered me eternal life through His Son, Jesus.

"But God demonstrates his own love for us in this: While we were still sinners, Christ died for us" (Romans 5:8). "For God so loved the world that he gave his one and only Son, that whoever believes in him shall not perish but have eternal life" (John 3:16). I believed that God loved me. I believed that God's Son, Jesus, took the punishment that I deserved and paid it Himself.

"That he was buried, that he was raised on the third day according to the Scriptures" (1 Corinthians 15:4). I believed that Jesus died on the cross to pay for my sins and that He rose from the dead.

"For it is by grace you have been saved, through faith—and this not from yourselves, it is the gift of God—not by works, so that no one can boast" (Ephesians 2:8-9). I realized there was nothing I could do to earn my way to heaven. I believed what He said was true, and I placed my trust in Him.

God loves you, too. He wants to be a part of your life. He made the way through His Son, Jesus Christ. All you have to do is put your trust in Him. You are an eternal being, created in the image of God. God alone offers the hope of eternal life through His Son, Jesus. Place your trust in Him and receive the gift of the forgiveness of your sins and the hope of eternal life.

Dear God, I know that I am a sinner. Please forgive me for my sin. I believe that You sent your Son Jesus to die on the cross to pay for my sins. I believe that He died, was buried, and that you raised Him from the dead on the third day. I place my trust in Jesus as my personal Lord and Savior. Please lead and guide me. Amen.

"That if you confess with your mouth, 'Jesus is Lord,' and believe in your heart that God raised him from the dead, you will be saved" (Romans 10:9). Jesus said, "I tell you the truth, whoever hears my word and believes him who sent me has eternal life and will not be condemned; he has crossed over from death to life" (John 5:24).

If you have made this decision, tell someone. Get a copy of the Bible, and start reading it. If you don't know where to start, you can turn to the Book of John and learn more about Jesus. Ask God to lead you. He is with you and promises to never leave you. You are the recipient of His great love and forgiveness, eternal life, and a living hope that will never perish.

Endnotes

[1] Melloni, June L. *Melloni's Pocket Medical Dictionary: Illustrated*. New York: Parthenon Pub. Group, 2004. *eBook Collection (EBSCOhost)*. Web. 12 Mar. 2014. 2162.

[2] Melloni, June L. *Melloni's Pocket Medical Dictionary: Illustrated*. 1032.

[3] Melloni, June L. *Melloni's Pocket Medical Dictionary: Illustrated*. 580.

[4] National Institute of Mental Health *NIH Publication No. 11-3561, Revised 2011*. *www.nimh.nih.gov*. http://www.nimh.nih.gov//index.shyml. (1/26/14).

[5] National Institute of Mental Health, *Depression*. *www.nimh.nih.gov*. *http://www.nimh.nih.gov//index.shtml*. (1/31/14).

[6] National Institute of Mental Health, *Depression*. *www.nimh.nih.gov*. *http://www.nimh.nih.gov//index.shtml*. (1/31/14).

[7] National Institute of Mental Health, *Depression*. *www.nimh.nih.gov*. *http://www.nimh.nih.gov//index.shtml*. (1/31/14).

[8] Dwight L. Carlson, *Why Do Christians Shoot Their Wounded? : Helping (Not Hurting) Those with Emotional Difficulties* (Downers Grove, Ill.: InterVarsity Press, 1994), 37.

[9] Carlson, *Why Do Christians*, 94–95.

[10] Carlson, *Why Do Christians*, 59, 74–76. In his book, Dr. Carlson discusses many contributing factors to depression. I mention these eight specifically to point out that there are physical contributing factors that can lead to depression.

[11] National Institute of Mental Health, *Depression. www.nimh.nih.gov. http://www.nimh.nih.gov//index.shtml*. (1/31/14).

[12] Timothy R. Jennings, *The God-Shaped Brain: How Changing Your View of God Transforms Your Life* (Downers Grove, Ill.: InterVarsity Press, 2013) 233.

[13] Jennings, *The God-Shaped Brain*(233-234).

[14] Taken from Halley's Bible Handbook by Henry H. Halley © 1965 by Henry H. Halley. Used by permission of Zondervan *www.zondervan.com*, 438.

[15] ²G. Campbell Morgan, *The Gospel According To Matthew* (Old Tappan, New Jersey: Fleming H. Revell Company, 1929), 131-132.

[16] ³C.H. Spurgeon, *All Of Grace* (Springdale, Pennsylvania: Whitaker House, 1983), 77.

[17] ⁴C.H. Spurgeon, *All Of Grace* (Springdale, Pennsylvania: Whitaker House, 1983), 76.

[18] ⁵John Bunyan, *Grace Abounding To The Chief Of Sinners* (Greenville, South Carolina and Belfast, Northern Ireland: Ambassador Publications), 59-60.

[19] Edited by Lee Gratiss, *The Sermons of George Whitelield, Volume II* (Wheaton, Illinois: Crossway, 2012) 269.

[20] Edited by Lee Gratiss, *The Sermons of George Whitelield, Volume II* (Wheaton, Illinois: Crossway, 2012) 269.

[21] Edited by Lee Gratiss, *The Sermons of George Whitelield, Volume II* (Wheaton, Illinois: Crossway, 2012) 269.

[22] John Bunyan, *The Pilgrim's Progress* (Peabody, Massachusetts: Hendrickson Publishers, 2004) 54-55.

[23] Larry J. Michael *Spurgeon On Leadership: Key Insights for Christian Leaders from the Prince of Preachers* (Grand Rapids, Michigan: Kregel Publications 2003) 194.

[24] Center for Disease Control. Suicide, Facts at a glance. *www.cdc.gov. www.cdc.gov/violenceprevention/pdf/suicide-datasheet-a.pdf.* (9/25/13)

[25] National Alliance on Mental Health. Suicide, *Mental Illness.* Reviewed by Ken Duckworth, M.D., and Jacob L. Freeman, M.D., Jan.2013. *www. nami.org. www.nami.org/Content/Navigation/Menu/Inform_yourself/ About_Mental_Illness/By_Illness/Suicide.htm.* (1/31/14).

[26] U.S. Department of Health and Human Services (HSS) Office of the Surgeon General and National Action Alliance for Suicide Prevention. *2012 National Strategy for Suicide Prevention: Goals and Objectives for Action.* Washington, DC: HSS, September 2012. p116 (1/31/14).

[27] Albert Y. Hsu, *Grieving a Suicide: A Loved One's Search for Comfort, Answers & Hope* (Downers Grove, Ill.: InterVarsity Press, 2002), 81.

[28] Matthew Henry, *Matthew Henry's Commentary on the Whole Bible* (Peabody, Massachusetts: Hendrickson Publishers, Seventh printing- March, 1997), 1624.

[29] Hsu, *Grieving a Suicide: A Loved One's Search for Comfort, Answers & Hope,112.*

[30] Ed Stetzer, "Mental Illness and the Church: New Research on Mental Health from LifeWay Research," *Lifeway Research.* September 17, 2013. *Christianity Today. www.christianitytoday.com* (1/31/14).

[31] Henry, *Matthew Henry's Commentary on the Whole Bible,* 741.

[32] Henry, *Matthew Henry's Commentary on the Whole Bible,* 741.